College Bound

How to Save and Budget Your Money to a Debt-Free Graduation

By T. Seay Gant

For:

Irene, Mattie, Andrew, and Fletcher Jr.

<u>Acknowledgements</u>

Father, Mother, God, Thank you for your grace and mercy. I'm truly blessed to live to see another day.

Thank you to my wonderful mother, Mary. You have brought me into a world with love and a mountain of financial education. It is because of your voice and encouragement, I am who I am today. To my role models, Lynnette and Sheree, thank you for being my beautiful, loving, sisters. I will always be grateful for your guidance and strength. To the Seay Family, Aunt Diane and Aunt Mary, Uncle John, Uncle Tony, Uncle Roy, and Uncle Johnnie as well as my 90+ Grandmother, Hattie, thank you for your love and support throughout my childhood. Thank you for helping me to remember the goodness of my Father. To the Williams Family, Thank you to my Aunt Linda, Aunt Alpheia, Aunt Pearl, and Uncle James (both of you), Derrick, Rodney, and Uncle Gerome for all the support you gave me while attending college. Thank you, to my 90+ Grandfather, Walter. You are truly the Vine for our family!

To the incredible young people in my life, Mariah, Nicholas, Alliyah, Andre, and the students I tutored over the years. You gave me hope that young people love to learn about math and money! Keep my lessons and use them to write your own future. To my cousins, Grover, John, Fletcher III, Sharmon, Paula, and my many other extended family members, thank you for showing me to follow my goals and becoming my own boss while pursuing financial opportunities. To Annette, Glynn, Veronice, Tiffany, Joseph, KaToya, and the entire Gant and Russell Family, thank you for welcoming me into your homes and loving me as your own. I appreciate your kindness and fellowship. To Terra, Mellonie, Rejoyce, Malecia, Danielle, Alondra, Cerissa, Misity, Adrienne, and all of my other girlfriends in Atlanta and Dallas, Thank you for believing in me when others doubted my talents and skills. I'm truly grateful for the love and friendship we have shared over the years.

To the air that I breathe, My Husband, Valdez, Thank you for your patience with me asking you so many questions, supporting my dreams, and loving me unconditionally. I love you.

Table of Contents

College Bound

How to Save and Budget Your Money to a Debt-Free Graduation

<u>Chapter 1: Early Years of Money Lessons and Influence</u>

My parents taught me how to get ahead in life when my options were limited, not only by their conduct as thrifty professionals, but also through the basic beliefs and principles they instilled within me. While I did visit my father and his side of the family occasionally, my childhood mostly took place in a single parent home. So while my childhood was an adventure—my mom had to juggle money and bills at times to make sure all was paid by the end of the month. I always had everything I wanted and needed because of the money-handling principles I learned from my parents.

For example, my father taught me an important lesson when I was in high school and trying to figure out a college major. He said, "You do what you are good at, not what you like. You do what you like when you have paid off your debt doing what you are good at." I still live by this quote as an adult when I make decisions about debt and finances.

Education was of first and foremost importance to my parents. If I had all As and maybe one B, I was able to do pretty much anything a little girl in southwest Atlanta desired.

I also learned from my siblings about money. As children, my sisters and I had two primary responsibilities: to get good grades in school and to respect our elders. My two sisters are older than I am, so they were also my first exposure to working and going to school. While in high school they could afford extracurricular activities because they paid for those things themselves. They paid their own way to play in the band, participate on the drill team, and march at half time with the high school band with the flag corp. I always loved math, so I learned from their example and frequently bought things I enjoyed with my own money.

I was also exposed to owning and operating a small business very early in life. My grandmother was a domestic worker, and my grandfather operated a landscaping business—which he still owns at the ripe young age of ninety-two! I saw firsthand the flexibility of working directly with customers. My grandparents' businesses gave them control over their time and money. My grandparents created opportunities for themselves through these businesses. Any loans needed for lawn supplies, for example, were based on a trust established with many of my grandfather's clients. His clients wanted to help grow his business by referring him to other friends and family for landscaping services. Back in those days, many black businesses were unable to obtain conventional loans through a bank, so most successful operations relied on a good name and solid relationships to receive money and grow. These experiences and lessons exposed me to the world of creating wealth, saving wisely, living within my means, and owing the least amount of debt as possible.

Throughout my childhood years and into my early teens, my parents influenced my money-handling spirit by working technical and corporate jobs. They taught me that it is difficult to live on one source of income and adequately save a good amount of money at the same time. Thus, I developed the idea that most working adults in my family should learn, start, and work a side job (or build another business) to build up their savings. This main philosophy–to always have other means of extra income—taught me how to overcome the limits of earning just one salary.

Multiple streams of income, as a concept, also revealed that I could lead myself to financial freedom because I knew I controlled both my spending power and my freedom to explore other opportunities. I had a part-time job when I was a teen, but I constantly looked for other avenues to make income that also would not interfere with my education. These opportunities gave me the chance to apply the principles I had learned as a child as well as the chance to see just how powerful the role money plays in our lives. I learned to save and make wise choices in a very real and practical way.

These activities prompted many conversations about money around the dinner table. My family and I always ate dinner around the same time at the dining room table. My mother did not care for eating in front of the T.V. because she believed we needed to talk about our day.

My sisters frequently brought their money situations into those conversations to discuss a variety of topics (e.g. how to pay for school activities on a part-time budget, etc.). My mother showed us how much money we could make each month after we paid the activity fees and other expenses. (Note: This is a good activity you can use as a parent to teach your kids how to control their time and money.)

This example of basic transactions showed us that if we wanted to participate in certain activities, then we had to determine not only how much we valued those activities, but also how much time, energy, and money those activities would demand from us. My sisters and I learned to see how a part-time job was not always enough, and it taught us to be creative with how we earned money. We worked side jobs like babysitting and helping senior family members run errands to earn extra cash. We quickly learned that expenses in high school often exceeded the money we made at our part-time jobs, and that side jobs are almost essential to effective money management.

I remember one conversation about money between my parents and siblings had one night at the dinner table. We discussed how to be successful in a career and how to get there with little to no debt.

Debt became an issue in my household when I was in middle school and my mother became a single parent of three girls. My mother provided for us and showed us the value of saving and making a dollar stretch to your benefit. We rallied as a family. We used to clip coupons; my sisters would do odd jobs such as babysitting and hairstyling, and would often work part-time after school to pay for extra school activities. This experience, and my mother working hard to support us, was a big lesson on how money really works. The foundational money principles I carry with me today were largely established in those conversations and experiences with my mother and sisters.

Many families do not speak about money to their children, and often many details about money are not discussed. Very few people know, for example, how important it is to own a home, how to save and invest in 401Ks (and other accounts), how to have adequate insurance coverage, and basic financial habits that prepare for the future.

The rare opportunity I had to learn from my parents has helped me make wise financial decisions ever since I graduated from college. Everything I know and practice as an adult came from my experience, from occasionally learning the hard way, and from the triumphs of using best principles—and it is my hope to pass along what I know to you in the coming pages.

Chapter 2: First Job in High School and/or College

I received my first job when I was eleven or twelve. I walked to an insurance adjuster's office each week, picked up some documents, and delivered them to my mother's employer. The company appreciated this because it saved time and money; for one, the receiving business did not have to wait a long time for these documents to arrive in the mail, and two, both parties saved on postage going back and forth. (This was before email saved everyone from sending everything through the Post Office.)

This job paid between fifteen and twenty dollars each week. I thought I was rich! I was always excited on Fridays because I could do the task and talk with the employees in the insurance adjuster's office. The only part I did not like about the job was that the pay became very inconsistent. This taught me a very important lesson: always finalize work details (as well as payment details) through a formal agreement *before* you accept a job.

This is when my mom helped me open my first savings account at a local bank. I needed fifty dollars to open the account, so it took me about a month to earn enough for the initial deposit. I had my first experience of control over my finances as a 12-year-old, and the feeling of ownership that came with it was amazing. Still, since the paychecks of an amateur carrier were inconsistent, I was always on the lookout for other means of income.

A few years later when I turned fifteen, I was blessed with a car and a driver's permit, so I began to work two jobs. Not only did I work a job in retail, but I also charged a low fee to drive my friends from place to place in our local area—a shared ridership before Uber was a thing!

My retail job was with a retail giant. Back in that day, this was a very typical job for a lot of high school students, and minimum wage was the norm. I kept this job all through high school and into my first two years of college. I usually worked only on the weekends because my mother wanted me to enjoy some school activities during the week and make money on the weekends. I remember

I made just over four dollars an hour with no benefits—unless you count the 10 percent employee discount. This discount came in handy whenever it helped me pay for any school items I needed.

In fact, it was this side hustle that provided for my expenses throughout high school and into college. My financial needs in high school were not that expensive because I was blessed to be in a home that provided all my needs very well. My greatest expenses were for gas (to get to school and work), car maintenance, all my school-related expenses, and—as a young woman—monthly hair maintenance. Figure 2.1 shows how I managed to pay for all those expenses despite earning mere minimum wage.

Figure 2.1

Description	Calculation	Final pay
Pay from part-time job	$4.25 x (14-15 hrs./week)	Weekly pay avg $60
Total pay for the month		= $240
- Save per month	10% to 20%	= ($48)
- Gas per month	$10 to $15 a week	= ($60)
- Senior fees/prom/ senior trip	Divide by 9 save to pay in April	= ($650)/9 = $72-75 per month

Some of the expenses I had to pay for while in high school are listed below:

High School Expenses

- Senior dues
- Prom fees
- S.A.T. & A.C.T. test fees
- My first computer
- Dial-up Internet access

Many of my colleagues worked part-time jobs in high school and college—and tried to manage money—much like myself.

My husband, now a successful math professor and engineer, worked for a pizza chain part-time while attending high school. He also participated in school activities such as band and football, and maintained a 3.6 grade point average at the same time.

My oldest sister, now a retired army sergeant, worked throughout high school. Today, she advises young people who currently work while attending school to work only in the summers—or have a work study—to dedicate maximum time for schoolwork. If she had to do it all over again, she said she would have worked less and enjoyed school more.

Chapter 3: Money Education Basics

As a young child, my parents taught me the importance of homeownership because they believed it was a gateway to obtaining wealth. I knew while I was in college that I wanted to graduate and become a homeowner directly afterwards. Upon graduation, I used the money basics I had been taught to help me acquire my first home at the age of twenty-three. I purchased my house five months before I graduated with my bachelor's degree.

Early on, I made the decision that I would live off cash and have little debt for as long as I attended college. This was a major reason why I could experience homeownership at such a young age. I had friends in college who could not afford a home because they had such a large debt-to-equity ratio due to their college loan debt. My friends also did not have money to put down the typical 3-5 percent on a mortgage. (It was easy to apply for first-time homebuyer programs in the 90's, as long as you had good credit; even if you did not have a lot of money, you could still apply as long as your income-to-debt ratio was below a particular percentage—so that was what I did. More on this later.)

In this chapter, I am going to explain how I saved for a down payment and minimized my debt while I was a full-time student.

Unfortunately, many basic money lessons (e.g. how much you need for a down payment, how housing insurance and property taxes impact your monthly mortgage, and which type of home loan is the best to get) were not explained to me until I was in college. Still, I combined what I learned as I grew up with what I was taught in school, and I made the best use of both sets of lessons to reach my wealth-building goals. I understood my upfront bills, developed my goals of saving in a 401K, and growing my career after a debt-free undergraduate education. This information provided a general finance knowledge base that created a large number of options for the future, and I want to help you have the same options—or better options—as a result of reading this book.

If you are a young teenager or young adult who is thinking about your financial future, this is the time and opportunity to think about things you like (i.e. a chance to review what you are good at as well as whether the path for a career or business relates to the goals that you desire for yourself or not). My family was made up of strong influences in math, engineering, and economics, and these influences shaped my early interests and the path I chose in college as well as my career. Financially, I set goals to live debt free on a comfortable salary and live in an affordable city that had low living costs. I researched different types of engineers as well as business roles that required education beyond an undergraduate degree. I also connected and built mentor relationships with some of my part-time managers while working in high school. They gave me advice on how to set goals, how to manage time, and many other skills that helped me to ask questions that lead to growth and opportunities.

The most basic finance activity that is often overlooked is balancing a check book. I know we live in the digital age where we can use digital apps to manage our checking accounts, but there is nothing like putting pen to paper to see how much is left in your account. In high school, I was taught about debts and credits, and how a balance sheet works for a small business. I started using a checkbook register to manage how much I took out in cash, spent on gas, and other basic needs. This was the beginning of the use of debit cards and you would think this would make things that much easier for people to manage their money in their account. Not so much. Many people still "feel" they know the correct amount in their checking account when they use their debit card. I started using my debit card in conjunction with my check register to keeping receipts and matching each receipt to the checkbook register. Then, I would reconcile the check book register to my account over the phone.

Today I do all this online. After I go over what I have in my register and compare it to what the bank has online in my account, I then see if I have enough money to get me through another week of gas or spending on school events.

Back then, if I didn't have enough money, I would typically reduce my driving for the week (if possible) by combining errands or making more side money from taking friends around the area. I would then place this money in my savings account to start my "little" emergency fund. It was a very small amount maybe about fifty dollars a month. These fundamentals gave me a great foundation in high school.

Young people will best understand and remember the value of a dollar when they manage their own money on their own. When I was younger, many of my friends received an allowance. I had no idea what this was or why it was given to my friends. Many of my friends received an allowance by completing chores around the house such as washing dishes, mowing the lawn, and babysitting a sibling. This was a strange concept to me because my mom used chores to teach me how to keep clean and that I should be thankful I had a house to live in. However, I did sometimes receive money for good grades and chores. This was not an often occurrence. Many parents in the 1980s in my neighborhood felt the same way about chores as my mother did; they believed chores were their children's duties for living in those homes. I remember those kids who received allowances began to consistently decrease after a period of time. Many young people felt they were owed money, when actually this was a kind gesture from parents to show their children money management.

One option to introduce and manage money for children and teens is to get a debit card from your local credit union or local bank. My credit union has a debit card just for children that allow parents to control the account from their smartphones. For example, parents can either limit their children's spending habits by choosing which stores their children can purchase from or allow full spending power as the children becoming teenagers. The debit card can also be deactivated by a smart device if the card is lost or stolen. This allows flexibility and control for parents while they teach their children to become more responsible and how to keep up with their own money. This is also a good way to pay out allowances to children. You don't have to worry about cash or going to the bank. You can simply transfer funds to the child's account and receive alerts about the child's spending habits in a report. Some banks or credit unions even offer a trial period just in case your family is not ready for the total responsibilities or not caught up on the learning curve of technology.

This is also a good way to show young people what it takes and required to earn money, save money, and manage what you have each week, month, or just for that moment! One example I experienced personally was being rewarded for good grades while in middle school. If I received an "A" on my report card in a subject I would receive a twenty-dollar bill for each "A". Talk about incentive as a preteen! I was also rewarded for Bs, but never for Cs. My parents believed Cs were basic or standard, but often told me they were proud that I tried my best. So with that standard, I would constantly strive for As and Bs.

Once my parents started to reward me for good grades, my mother demonstrated the concept of learning the value of making good grades in reference to the time I spent studying. (See Figure 3.1.)

Figure 3.1

Class Grade	Time invested	Cash received	Money able to save
A	3-4 hours per week	$20	$80 per quarter
B	2-3 hours per week	$10	$30-$40 per quarter

My mother described that the amount of money I could earn correlated directly with the amount of time I invested on homework and studying for tests. Thus, if I wanted a new sweater my mom explained that a thirty-dollar sweater would take about 40-50 hours of schoolwork within a quarter to earn thirty dollars at the end of the term for one class. By adding a dollar value to each study/schoolwork hour, I was able to make early decisions as a middle schooler on what the value was worth. This forced me to always consider whether the item I wanted was actually worth that amount of time. That lesson continued to come up in my life and in school, especially when I started purchasing more of what would last a long time and less of what was just a fashion fad.

Giving Children an Understanding of Money

Family conversations, part-time work, and learning the value of money at a young age are all methods that ultimately help young people prepare for college and adult life. As early as the preteen years, young people can have a greater understanding just by talking about financial matters at the dinner table. Basic financial concepts such as debts, credits, receipts, and managing an allowance all provide a foundation to common sense money education. If preteen babysitters understand that babysitting two hours at ten dollars per hour gets them twenty dollars to use towards a high school event, then they will be much disciplined to handle it well. The basic knowledge to manage that twenty dollars, as well as value the time spent to make that money, causes them to have the goal of attending the school events and making a dream into a reality. This lesson allows the young person to gain firsthand experience for the potential college and adult years to come.

I learned about basic credits and debits using a business calculator and real-world examples as part of an elective I took (it was a banking class) while a junior in high school. With music technology, students learned that buying a song from a music service creates a debit in their online account. However, students also learned that a credit is when their parents add money to their music account or to a prepaid debit card. These are examples of how technology can help manage debits and credits without necessarily using receipts, checkbooks, or any other type of reconciliation tools.

While in college another friend Johnny O. had many ups and downs while providing for himself and going to school at the same time. He had credit card debt, worked several years in retail, and supported family members who constantly borrowed money from him. He graduated with debt but felt confident that he would have a job as soon as he completed his classes. He went on two interviews after graduation. He felt so confident and proud about his interviews that he went and bought a brand-new Nissan Maxima. He said, "I got it made! I'm going to get offers from both jobs!" As time moved on and car payments became due, he never received any job offers from those two interviews. Not only that, but he also did not get any offers from any other prospects! He was stunned. He tells this story to many of his commercial clients today. It serves as his testimony about why you should not live with debt while you attend—or even after you graduate—from college. Today, he is a successful commercial banker that writes loans for several commercial businesses. He now is debt free after working together with his wife for many years to create a debt-free lifestyle.

Another friend of mine had to find other ways to pay for her college expenses. Amanda O. discovered she had a serious illness and needed to take a leave of absence to seek medical treatment. She was previously awarded scholarships and grants and didn't want to lose this money while on medical break. Amanda O. called the Financial Aid Department and asked for her scholarships and grants to be placed on hold until she returned. The school held her funds, and she was able to use them upon her return. She resumed her education after a three-month absence for kidney failure treatment. She received her bachelor of arts degree a couple of years later, after she received a new kidney from her brother.

Once while I was tutoring tenth graders in a local school district in Texas, I had a conversation about loans with my students. Mainly the conversation involved student loans, debt, and credit cards. In a group of five students, the main consensus was to not get student loans to pay for college. When I asked them why they believed this, they all replied, "It's just bad, but we don't know why" I proceeded to ask, "What about credit card debt?" They all looked confused. It was never clearer to me than it was in that moment about how often young people are completely blind to the concepts of debt and loans even before they first walk onto a college campus.

One of the first experiences I had when I stepped on my college campus was the chance to get free "stuff" if you signed up for a credit card. This "stuff" included all kinds of things such as T-shirts, coffee cups, foam cup holders, and on and on. At this time, I really felt like an adult with my personal line of credit. When I told my mom that I had signed up for one she quickly told me to cancel the credit card. The reason she gave was because the interest rate was well over 20 percent, and that it would take years to pay off any of the charges. This made me wonder, "What value is an item if I have to pay an additional amount in interest for it?"

That question helped me make a great financial decision over a typewriter. I needed a digital typewriter to type my papers when the computer lab was closed on campus. While the cost for a new one was $125, I knew it was a valuable purchase not only because I would be doing a great amount of typing on it, but also because I knew I would not have additional interest to pay. The choices I had included:

1) Use a high interest credit card and try to pay the total amount within six months at twenty dollars per month (plus interest)
2) Pay eighty dollars up-front and borrow forty-five dollars from a family member (with no interest)

3) Pay $125 in full in exchange not be able to save up any money for the next 3-4 months

I decided on option three. That digital typewriter lasted almost five years before I bought my first personal computer. This decision enabled me to save time because I had the equipment with me in my dorm/apartment. I could complete my schoolwork on my digital typewriter at any time whereas the computer lab closed at 10:00 p.m. on weekdays and at 6:00 p.m. on weekends. Not only that, but I was also able to quickly save up my money in the long run because I let many of my classmates use it to type their papers for a fee.

Don't get me wrong I had a credit card for emergencies that I rarely used; however, I went through a tedious selection process before making a final decision. I decided to go with my local bank credit card as my first student credit card, which had a 12 percent interest rate.

While I attended college, I worked at a regional bank as a floating teller. This is someone who can work during peak hours and travel to other bank branches at busy times during the day. I received all kinds of credit card advice from coworkers, branch managers, and other financial specialists about how to manage credit card debt and how to use debt for your benefit. The benefits they told me to look for were manageable credit lines, and most importantly, a low interest rate. MasterCard and Visa offered very similar benefits to each other as far as interest rates and reward options were concerned. I chose the regional bank's Visa card, which had a credit limit of $2000. At the time, I thought 12 percent was a great rate; however, after a few months I discovered I had family members with $10,000 lines of established credit with interest rates as low as 3.5 percent. "Wow!" I thought. I can't wait to get out of school and have established credit! But why wait? I could start establishing my credit while in college.

I know some of you are wondering, why not American Express? During that time, you had to have a certain salary and credit rating before American Express (or Amex as it is called today) would consider issuing you a credit card. Also, Amex was more of a card whereas the balance on the card was due at the end of each month. (Today we consider this a charge card.) Basically, it would allow a purchase but you had to pay it in thirty days. The interest rate was mostly nonexistent—as in it was considered late if you did not pay in those 30 days. Now, Amex works just as Visa and MasterCard as a true credit card that holds balances and has an annual interest rate.

In deciding on the lowest interest rate, one would think this is as easy as picking the lowest rate. As a college student, this is more about beginning the journey of establishing a credit history.

Now, there are cards that give cash back and cards that give points for groceries, gas, food, and other purchases (which are all things a college student will need). The interest rate really depends on the bank rate and prime rate. Also, the interest rate may depend on if you have any credit before going to college. For instance, a cell phone bill with a monthly music-streaming service, or a bank account with a good history are both examples of items that young teens and college students can use to establish a credit history.

Nowadays, several banks have credit cards especially for college students. Some of the benefits include 3 percent cash back rewards on things such as gas and groceries (for a limited time) and 1 percent cash back (after the introductory limited time). Many of these bank cards have an introductory rate of 0 percent, but the interest rate increases significantly into a range that often exceeds at least 12.5 percent. This is mostly based upon your credit score. While this is a good start for a college credit card, another option is to consider a credit card from a credit union.

Credit unions may not offer many of the benefits and rewards as commercial banks; however, one of the best features of credit unions is that they usually offer a very low interest rate. By far credit union interest rates are generally 6-7 percent less than traditional banks, which allow you to pay more towards the debt than just the interest.

Other options that can help a college student save money include no annual fees, no balance transfers, and no cash advance fees. An annual fee is usually a fee just for possessing a credit card. Depending upon the credit card, some annual fees can be over one hundred dollars a year. Balance transfer fees may be added when a student consolidates higher interest credit cards to lower interest cards which, again, can be paid off faster with a lower interest rate. This allows the student to pay off all debt that is accumulated during the college years.

Finally, the most important reason to have a credit card while in college is for emergencies. If you are away from home, this is very important as emergencies can come up—anything from additional car repairs, health emergencies, and unexpected school expenses. If cash is needed for emergency funds, cash advances through a credit card are an option (e.g. a flat tire). I had a flat tire in a snowstorm while attending undergrad. The technician only accepted cash; I had twenty dollars on me and was going to receive my paycheck later in the week. He took me to the nearest A.T.M. to get cash before he changed my tire. Thankfully, all I needed was my tire plugged thus I saved about one hundred dollars on the total expense of the tire. The interest rate and the fees for cash advances are mostly over 21 percent (so this is where credit unions really separate themselves from their competition). Some credit unions offer credit cards with no fees on cash advances, though they still maintain the higher interest rate. This benefit can help save a large amount of money that can accumulate over your college years.

Chapter 4: Saving and Managing Money While in High School

Growing up in the Southeast United States, I had many expenses in high school that enabled me to have success and good grades throughout high school. Many of them—such as standardized testing fees, tutoring costs, special preparatory courses, and many others—were not paid by school districts as they are today. Presently, high school students have a head start with the tools they need—including weekly savings, extra help outside of school, and controlling expenses—not only to have a successful financial life while in college, but also to go to college debt free and graduate with no additional debt.

As savings was explained before, a weekly savings for a high school student can be the difference between extra money for student needs versus no money as a result of reliance on debt to fund everyday school expenses.

When I had my retail job while in high school, I set aside a basic amount per month for needs outside of my possible wants. I opened a student savings account for twenty-five dollars at a small local bank. If the local commercial banks in your area do not offer student-focused accounts or low initial deposits, then credit unions and online banks may be viable options to consider.

When opening a student savings account, the student (and possibly a parent) should review the monthly budget. The budget should include how much income is made per month through the student's part-time job, allowance, etc., as well as the student's expenses that may occur on a monthly basis. Such expenses as sports equipment, band fees, class trips, school uniforms, and other costs can all be a part of a high school student's accumulated debt over a four-year period.

I opened my first savings account in the ninth grade, and set my basic savings goal at fifty dollars per month. Once I started to drive and had my own car, I increased the amount to about $75-100 per month. I was able to save more during my sophomore year because I started to drive, and therefore was able to work more frequently.

Along with those increased savings, my mother also introduced the concept of tithing (i.e. the practice of giving 10 percent of your income to your church), and so I began to tithe routinely for the local church where my family and I attended ever since I was in elementary school. For me—and according to the Christian faith—this practice begins a spirit of helping others. However, this is ultimately a decision that parents and students should discuss together in order for the student to handle it wisely. As a teenager, I gave consistently for years, but only began to tithe 10 percent once I became an adult. The ability to give to others and to a faith I believe in has been a great honor, and has been truly satisfying throughout my years of giving. I can only hope every student will eventually help others during high school, college, and after graduating debt free.

As a young person going away to college or living away from home, a "needs" budget list is a must. Overall, there are many everyday items that are necessary just to maintain hygiene and provide convenient eating solutions for those intense study periods during time-restricted testing schedules. Three main priorities I had were grooming/hair needs, gas for my car, and extra snacks or easy-to-prepare home meals. When I attended college, I always, *always* had my hair looking nice. (Why did this matter, you ask? For me, it was always important, no matter what my budget was, to maintain my hair and keep it constantly fixed because I viewed it as a small reward for working and going to school daily.) I had stylists I went to near campus and others near my Mother's home—an hour away from campus. (By the way, I occasionally drove back home in order to wash clothes on the weekends to save from spending anything at the laundromat. This was another way I would generally "pamper" myself, about every six to eight weeks.)

Some friends of mine rewarded themselves for making good grades with similar grooming perks such as manicures, pedicures, massages, or shopping trips for specialty items like popular sneakers.

Then, there are grooming needs that do not qualify as splurges but as necessities. Healthcare (while in college or technical school), for example, can come from your parents' healthcare coverage or simply from a part-time job that provides healthcare benefits. However, many students rely on the school facilities or a local clinic. I, for example, received biannual teeth cleanings at the nearby dental school for free! Young men often received haircuts in their dorm rooms for less money than the barber shop. My husband groomed on a budget by buying razors and shaving cream for $15, which helped him stay groomed on a budget for a year. Buying grooming items in bulk or at discount stores that sell personal hygiene items ultimately can save a good amount of money each month, enabling you to pay for other areas of needs. These are all examples of grooming on a budget.

When I first learned how to drive and received my first car, I was so excited to have my independence to go to school and my part-time job, as well as to earn gas money by taking my friends to different places. I received my first car at the age of fifteen, and I quickly learned that other expenses come as a result of owning a car. During this period of my life, gas was very inexpensive, so I charged my friends differing rates depending upon the miles and the time of day (and especially if I had to endure a lot of time in traffic). If it was on the weekend (which was rare), I would charge almost double my normal rate. This was a great way to earn extra money for gas and for all my high school functions. I could drive almost for free on the additional money. Another perk I discovered, as a result of receiving the free gas money, was the ability to use a gas card that came with cash back rewards, additional free gas rewards, as well as points rewards. A lot of young people today can use these rewards for such items as music gift cards, online stores gift cards, etc.

Another way to get money for car expenses is to operate popup car washes at your home, or even the local car wash self-service lot. Many people who have extra money (and little time to spare) will pay handsomely for someone to wash their cars. I know I also ran errands and grabbed bites to eat for my family to get free food and money when I was in high school.

Presently, there are many service apps that do these exact services. Some provide meal delivery for a fee and others provide mobile car washes that come to you to wash your car. When I did this it was just another income boost for gas. This provides teens and college students with many options to save money for gas or for snacks that curb those late-night study cravings.

High School Expenses

Most expenses during high school happen during your junior and senior years. If outside activities are involved with the student, then the additional expenses will accumulate over the years until high school graduation. These years are important as the student prepares for higher education in college or trade school. During this time in my life, I knew I wanted to be an industrial engineer, mainly because I loved science and math throughout school. (Of course, my major changed once I got in college, but I spent my high school years preparing for those classes.) In fact, I once completed two years' worth of math classes in one year (my sophomore year in high school). I completed Geometry and Algebra II in the same year so I could take Pre-Calculus my junior year, followed by A.P. Calculus my senior year. Since I chose to take an accelerated route to get ahead in math, I bought my expensive calculator and paid to take a S.A.T. /A.C.T. preparatory class at a nearby community college. The preparatory class was about $150 and another $25-50 for a book and workbook. In the past, schools did not provide funding for preparatory courses or any testing fees. Today, many school districts offer to pay for testing fees for the S.A.T. and the A.C.T. for initial tests as well as some application fees for college admissions. With local school districts offering to pay these high school fees, the savings for a college-bound student can amount to anywhere from $120-$150 (just for registration and fees). Also, there are opportunities for eleventh and twelfth graders to waive S.A.T. fees by qualifying for an income-based waiver. Then, there are some materials online to prepare for both standardized tests that can help students practice for free, which also provide a savings in fees for high school students. Finally, many public schools use class tutorials and advisement periods to practice test-taking through practice tests, which can prevent students from having to pay additional fees for tests they have to repeat. These savings make a great foundation for students when they start their freshman year.

One of my first major purchases besides a vehicle while I was in high school was a Texas Instruments (T.I.) graphing calculator (T.I.-80 model). As a junior in high school, I took Pre-Calculus and I knew higher-level math classes were in my future. This calculator cost about seventy-five dollars. That was a lot of part-time money I had to save and earn in order to buy what I needed. Today, T.I. still makes these multi-function calculators for about $125 to $150 depending on the complexity of the calculator's functions. This is an important money tip for high school students because students today can work around not having such an expensive calculator if they do not plan to take math courses above Algebra. However, many schools are promoting S.T.E.M. (Science, Technology, Engineering, and Math) courses for education which will require scientific calculators sooner than later. Today, apps on your cell phone can do many of the same functions as a graphing/scientific calculator and a business calculator. Of course, you need a reliable smartphone in order to operate those apps, which may cost more than $500 in and of itself. But this is an option I didn't have, and I believe this can save money in high school and college if your curriculum program requires advanced mathematics.

Another calculator I had to buy was a business calculator made by Casio. This specifically did business calculations such as net present value, amortization schedules, and many others. My high school was a business magnet school, which meant some business-oriented elective courses such as banking and small business entrepreneurship. This exposure to business basics in high school sparked my interest in pursuing my undergraduate degree in business management after changing from engineering.

In today's society, a high school student greatly benefits from having a personal computer. Many school districts have computer labs, or even laptops and tablets, that students can use throughout the school year to complete assignments in school and at home. The convenience of having a desktop or laptop at home, however, gives students flexibility and other advantages towards better results in school. I did not have a computer until after I graduated with my undergraduate degree, and I used a typewriter (with a preview screen) during my first couple years of college. By my senior year (the 5th year) I had purchased my first computer—from the now defunct store and brand—Compaq. It cost me over $1,100 for a monitor, C.P.U. (central processing unit), and keyboard. I had no money to buy a major computer outright, and decided to use a credit promotion of 12 months no interest. The ability to have my own desktop computer allowed me to work efficiently on schoolwork, both day and night. My first computer allowed me to focus well, and ultimately helped me finally graduate.

Other expenses that arise during your junior and senior years of high school are for fun activities such as senior dues, the prom, senior trips, and many others. Senior dues and senior proms really depend upon how active the student body is in planning outside activities as well as the parental support for these activities. Many senior fees include a class ring, a yearbook, class graduation t-shirt, and awards dinners for top-performing students and athletes.

Those last couple years of high school are some of the most memorable times of life. I still vividly remember being a part of the prom committee as well as my senior trip planning committee. I appreciated all the effort that made my experiences both fun and cost-effective. My senior-year trip (a night at Disney World with other students across America) cost about $500. This included the bus ride, food, admission to the park, and access to other sections of the Orlando park. Our chaperones were young, first-year teachers who volunteered in exchange for a free trip.

In addition, many schools today choose to incorporate college campus visits, community service events, and other activities that emphasize educational, cultural, and social benefits over excessively fun activities that hold little educational, cultural, or social value.
Finally, one of the most expensive costs is tutoring fees. There are many high schools that offer group tutorials such as A.V.I.D. (Advancement Via Individual Determination)

tutoring, or tutoring and advisement hours. If you want outside tutoring for your student, private tutoring companies can cost anywhere from $50-$100 an hour. Does this actually help your student? In my experience as a student and as a tutor, you are only successful when you put in maximum effort.

Effort is measured by the amount of time your student invests as well as the amount of energy your student puts forth while pursuing a high school diploma and a college degree. When I was in college, I was never able to afford tutoring. I remember I met with the Dean of Math and Sciences program about my Calculus 2 class. He told me to talk to my professor and ask if he would be able to provide me with help outside of class. Unfortunately, my professor did not view my questions as typical questions from class notes, so he suggested that I needed tutoring. I was initially excited to have specialized attention for my favorite subject. As I explained before, however, I was on a budget. Thus, any extra expenses had to be planned and accounted for months in advance. When I called the tutor my professor had recommended, I was told the cost would be $100 an hour! I was shocked and devastated. I could barely eat outside of sandwiches and tacos, so this expense was *well* over my budget. This became a major turning point in my school experience. I ultimately did not pass the class and I changed my major to business (in which I earned my BA).

Presently, students have many more free resources that support their need for tutoring such as group tutoring, graduate students who tutor for discounted rates, and online tutorial videos that can give step-by-step instructions on certain topics. These create opportunities for all students to be successful, and if you invest in your educational goals, the outcome can mean the difference between graduating with your desired degree and not achieving personal goals due to a lack of resources and money.

<u>Chapter 5: Managing Debt on a Budget</u>

Many parents are often unprepared for the living expenses that come along with attending college away from home. Some schools occasionally provide relief through partial scholarships or scholarships that only pay for tuition (with no aid for housing or additional expenses).

In this chapter I will provide examples of how big-ticket items (e.g. housing, transportation, food, etc.) affect both the accumulation and reduction of debt, both while in college and after graduation. These items greatly influence whether students graduates with zero debt or with a burden of debt.

A couple years ago I had a coworker friend (Phyllis) whose youngest daughter received a full-tuition scholarship to attend a private university. At first, my friend was over-the-moon proud that her daughter could attend such a prestigious school, but then she realized she had totally overlooked the enormous cost of living she was going to be charged for room and board. This cost alone put her in massive debt.

Figure 5.1

Expenses	On Campus living	Off Campus Living
Room and Board	$12500	$24000
Transportation	$6500	$7000

The chart above is an estimate of expenses for room and board as well as for transportation costs that can add significantly to a college student's debt over a span of four years.

By graduation day, Phyllis and her daughter together owed over $50,000 in bank loans. This money paid for all living expenses and most transportation expenses over the four years she attended college. Yes, she did save on tuition and some expenses due to her scholarship and working part time, but her future will begin with loans demanding roughly a 10 percent interest rate (depending upon how long it takes to pay her personal loans off). Phyllis and her daughter will likely have this debt count against their debt-to-equity ratio for 10-15 years or more. Unfortunately, this is not unusual. Many students now start their careers after they graduate from college with the odds stacked against them with debt.

I am often asked today how I was able to graduate debt free without paying for living expenses. I explain that I had a budget that accounted for every last financial expense of my college life. My budget for living expenses, transportation expenses, and food expenses have all made a difference for me ever since I finished college, and it can help you long after you graduate as long as you maintain a similar budget.

Many students dream about the experience of living away from home in a dorm or an off-campus apartment. During my freshman year, I shared a small 10x12-foot dorm room with one of my best friends from high school. It was a great experience, but it was also a learning experience.

After my freshman year, my roommate decided to have a dorm room all to herself. I had a decision to make: Do I share another dorm room with someone I don't know or do I fork over an additional $400-500 a semester for a private dorm room? I decided to get my own dorm with no roommate. This made my budget tighter, so my college experience also became much more restrictive. Both my savings goals and what I could and could not spend my money on were affected. This time became the most difficult period of my life. My eating budget was drastically cut, so I had to find other ways to cut my budget to accommodate living with the full costs of a dorm room. The items that helped in reducing my budget were laundry at my mother's house, buying inexpensive personal items and toiletries, and cooking and eating almost all of my meals in my room.

The first undergraduate college I attended was outside Atlanta, Georgia—a little more than an hour and half away from my mother's home where I grew up. I rarely traveled home during my freshman year because of the distance. Later, however, she sold that home to move closer to the city, so this cut about 30 minutes from my commute. I was able to travel home every weekend during my sophomore year, and I would always go home to do laundry.

Where I once had to spend at least four or five dollars for each load for laundry at school during my freshman year (which often included detergent, fabric softener, machine operation, and any other specialty item I needed to complete my laundry), for about three loads of clothes each week, I was then able to save all that money during my sophomore year.

My clothes were often very worn by the end of the day because I often walked to class, plus I always changed clothes to go to work in the evenings after I finished my classes. (I worked for a small bank in my college town, which also helped me save a tremendous amount of money.) By the time I transferred to my alumni school to graduate with my undergraduate degree, I had invested in a used washer and dryer (which lasted more than ten years), thus preventing me from spending hundreds of dollars at the laundromat.

Another area I had to change in my budget was removing excessive spending in exchange for money-saving habits. For example, I once discovered I purchased way too many personal items. I had a habit of buying paper cups, paper plates, throw-away napkins, premium juice boxes, and other convenience items. While I adjusted my spending habits by purchasing in bulk, I also started to buy reusable plastic cups, plates, and cutlery. By washing these items after each use, I was able to keep from spending weekly $10-15 per week on throw-away paper products. This adjustment also made me a more efficient shopper, as I would stretch my budget by shopping only once or twice a month. The lessons I learned in college about simple shopping habits continue to help my family save money and be more efficient even today.

As a student, I also decided to join on another family member's membership to a big warehouse club. This decision to buy detergent, cereal, and other toiletries in bulk allowed me to avoid paying for those items again for about three months at a time. Yes, this can be a little more money spent in the beginning, but after calculating the math (i.e. comparing prices and the term of usage), it was much more efficient to buy a surplus of items that you will always need and probably use routinely.

Figure 5.2

Toilet paper	Toothpaste
Laundry detergent	Vitamins
Fabric softener	Water
Snacks	Juice and/or soft drinks

Buying the items listed in Figure 5.2 (and others like them), will also lead to saving money on food and going out to eat.

My cousin gave me a small refrigerator that kept my water and juice cold, which cut my meal costs even more because I would just purchase the meal. (A drink would add about three dollars to your total bill, which could be an additional meal for a college student.) I also kept snacks such as yogurt in my mini fridge, which kept my food budget safe when I had to study overnight for upcoming tests. I also would buy small juice boxes that came twenty to a pack. The benefit of have juice boxes was they did not have to be refrigerated until I wanted to drink them, and with my mini fridge being so small, space was at a premium. Thus, I was able to keep them at room temperature in a small storage unit and a few in the fridge. These cost savings on food and supplies allowed me to keep more money in my pocket during the school year.

I also owned a (used) microwave that I got from my aunt. This concept of buying preowned products at a discount from family or close friends also helps you save a lot of money. My cousin passed along his mini fridge to me after he used it at the same university in one of his fraternity houses. I also had a small kitchenette in my dorm room, which was really a money saver for cooking and eating for about four years. I must admit, I did miss going out to eat, but I was thankful on graduation day that I had no debt from all those years of college.

School Fees

No matter how much you budget for school fees, books, access key codes, etc., any fees for school are a definite expense once you graduate high school and enter college or technical school. Every semester my books totaled at least $500 and that was 3-4 times a year! Luckily for today's student, you can buy access codes to access online textbooks. This is a better value. These books also provide the additional benefit of convenience, as they are frequently equipped with homework aids and can be uploaded to a mobile/electronic device. However, the student should still prepare a budget for school supplies. I mentioned earlier about supplies such as business calculators and graphing calculators, but there are also fees charged by the school that are outside basic tuition. These fees include activity fees, technology fees, and many others.

Activity fees include costs for intramural sports, organizations, club fees, and many other extra offerings outside of basic educational courses. I participated in going to football games as well as the student union while in college. This was a great way to meet other students outside the dorm and classrooms. Normally, these activities would each have a cost to participate, but we were given a budget by the school for providing free activities for the student body. The student union organization introduced me to my roommates in college. This was the start of friendships that we still enjoy today, more than twenty years later. Other fees such as lab fees are usually to replace lab equipment used during lab courses (e.g.

Biology Lab and Chemistry Lab). I broke several beakers while in my chemistry course. I passed the course but I suspected a bill was coming. Once I transferred and was about to graduate, I thought I would have to pay for those beakers to receive my diploma, but the Science Department told me it was already paid in my student fees that I pay every semester.

Many online textbooks have already replaced the traditional hard copy textbook, and these digital books often have access codes that unlock supplemental online material such as PowerPoint presentations, digital illustrations, and videos. In many classes, the access codes can cover several classes in a series (e.g. College Algebra 1 and 2).

Food Expenses

Another expense that can impact your college budget is food expenses. Yes, many students usually gain the classic "freshman fifteen" (gaining fifteen pounds during your first year as a student) as a result of new eating habits and leaving home. Many students' eating habits change due to a budget that cannot afford healthy foods. Also, if you are working and going to classes, you are most likely to eat at times that are late in the evenings or on-the-go between classes. I mostly ate canned foods and frozen meals; both were high in sodium and were not good for my overall health. I also had my fair share of tacos and pizza, so I gained maybe five pounds (since I constantly walked around campus to keep my parking space for the entire week). All that walking helped me gain muscle, but it also helped me save on gas since I was on a transportation budget!

While attending classes around lunchtime, I would have the opportunity to enjoy my favorite fast foods at the campus food court. These would include sandwiches from the popular sandwich shops, fried chicken from well-known fried chicken restaurants, and of course, my all-time favorite—pizza. The restaurants would have areas to eat outside and large dining areas with large windows to enjoy while eating with other students and spending time with friends. Most of the food court restaurants had value meals and specialty foods that can be great for a weekly "cheat" meal. My budget was usually about five dollars for a meal. That amount is a pretty normal standard today, as most fast food restaurants have a value menu where all of the choices are usually fewer than five dollars, and you can get a lot of different items for those five dollars. If I ever could not afford a full meal due to low funds, I would settle for a couple of tacos (at 29 cents each) and a cup of water. Cheap, but very good at the time. Of course, five dollars is not a lot for a meal, but there were times I had less than three dollars for a meal. If I could not get to my dorm room to eat a quick meal, my last resort was to grab something out of the vending machines around campus. Presently, vending machines now take debit and credit cards while charging an additional fee for items pulled out of those machines. This type of convenience can wreck a budget or be a welcome relief—just in time for hunger that strikes in the middle of a study night. The machines in the business school I attended even had cold sandwiches starting at two dollars that I could warm up in the student lounge microwave. Once again, not the healthiest option, but it did get me through most days when I was on campus.

During my freshman year in college a meal plan was attached to my room and board fees, which meant I had a meal ticket for breakfast, lunch, and dinner. While that sounds nice, it unfortunately added, on average, an additional $500-750 to the room and board fees. Once again, I had a decision to make. I always wanted to eat at the food courts which had popular fast food restaurants (because the food tasted better than what was in the cafeteria). By my second year, however, I decided to forego the meal plan and buy my own food. I often splurged once a week with a meal from one of the specialty restaurants as a luxury reward for working and going to school. There were also restaurants around campus that offered specials for college students. For instance, Tuesday nights were "15 cent wings" night at a favorite sports and wing bar. Another night of the week, the local Mexican restaurant had a special for three chicken tacos for three dollars. These deals helped me stay fed all the years I attended school. I lived on twenty-five dollars a week, and usually had leftover food for the next week. By walking all over campus and eating small portions of healthy and budget-friendly food, I was able to stay fit and stay within budget.

I had a roommate who worked for a buffet-style steakhouse as a waitress most weeknights while we attended college. While our roommate was at work, I would go to a local buffet steakhouse with my other two roommates. Each one of us saved about $5-7 from a previous payday, so we would pool our money together for a total of $18-21 and buys the all-you-can-eat family buffet. We ate like queens. This extended my budget for the week because I always saved my last plate for lunch the next day. We not only built lifelong friendships with one another, but we also helped each other ease the burden of eating on a budget.

If studying makes you hungry for snack food or junk food, you will likely succumb to your urges more often as you continue to pursue your education, and buying extra food can be expensive for the typical student. Many college graduates often speak of the "freshmen fifteen." This is the very common event—which may or may not be explained during your freshman year—of gaining an excessive amount of weight. I did not have this experience because I often snacked while studying instead of eating full meals. My husband survived his college study cravings with a food warehouse club membership card. This was also a great opportunity to sample snacks every week for free! Buying in bulk also helped him keep his costs down from because it kept him from buying expensive snack foods in smaller packaging. For instance, I would compare the cost of large bags of chips at the grocery store along with the individual snack bags in a variety snack box variety pack of chips (which usually had 15-20 different types of chips). Many times I saved anywhere from $2-3 total. I also got to choose from a larger selection of flavors by purchasing in bulk.

I know you are wondering, What about the membership fees? Well, my husband buys a fifty-dollar membership each year. This membership also provides discounts with gas as well. Many of these food discount warehouses usually have some of the least expensive gas prices in their areas.

Be warned, however, that there are negatives that can counter the savings of buying in bulk, especially if you buy too much. Even though you get more for your money, you still have to look at your cost of supplies (and other costs in your budget) so as to estimate if you can survive a semester of school without depleting your goods. For example, during high school, I ran track in the spring of my junior year. I had to limit how often I ate snacks to twice a day. My mom told me once the snacks were gone for the term, they were gone! This also helped keep my weight on target for my track goals and weigh-ins. Actually, most of my snacks would carry over to the next month, and my mom usually shopped at the membership club every other month or so. This was another idea that I used when I went off to college to help me save money for food and other college expenses.

Basically, students are presented with many, wide range of choices that comes with eating on campus or off campus. Most decisions about food will truly depend upon your financial availability as well as you budget for expenses and food.

Chapter 6: Life-Changing Expenses While in School

One very important lesson I learned from going to school without a lot of money was I had to make very hard decisions. This was when I really began to develop my spiritual growth through Bible study and daily prayer. I often was down to my last $1 and had to decide between paying for a school need or a personal need (e.g. eating cheap fast food). I soon learned how helpful it was to arrange a list of needs and wants (i.e. priorities) into categories using the questions in Figure 6.1 to make some of the toughest decisions I faced while attending college.

Figure 6.1

First Question	Second Question	Third Question
What I want to do?	What I might want to do?	What do I definitely not want to do?

Do I work more than 20 hours a week in exchange for less study time? Do I live on campus or off campus? Do I have a roommate to help with splitting the rent and other bills or live on my own? Do I lease or buy a car in full? New or used? All these questions affected my daily budget, my grades, and my future buying power.

The three decisions that affected my life the most while attending college were 1) apartment living, 2) leasing a car, and 3) working more hours to pay for living expenses.

That last decision (i.e. to work more hours) affected all aspects of my life while I attended college. I worked two part-time jobs while studying a full load of college classes. That decision came more out of necessity than from wanting to work 20-30 hours each week. Many of my college friends did not work during the school year, but they would work full-time every summer. Their grades reflected this choice also as most of them held steady at a B-average level. My junior year cumulative grade point average (G.P.A.) was barely above 2.5, as it got more and more difficult to work and achieve good grades. Many of my friends ended up graduating with a higher G.P.A. than I did because my choice to work resulted in a final G.P.A. of 2.8. The extra

20-25 hours of additional study time each week would have benefited my grades tremendously! In the present day, a student has more work options while in college, especially by coordinating class schedules with paid internships that compliment a student's degree.

Many of these internships are available through the student's university and/or companies that recruit at college job fairs. Companies open to internships for students with specific majors usually require a minimum G.P.A. and a work schedule of at least forty hours a week during school breaks. Many colleges host job fairs for companies and students during the Spring semester for graduating seniors and/or specific majors.

Another type of internship is known as a co-op (short for cooperative) program. This program lets students combine schoolwork together with a steady job (usually performed in the Summer and holiday breaks) in exchange for all expenses paid by the employer while the student goes to school. Almost every major has sponsoring co-ops today. Students who major in science, technology, engineering and math (S.T.E.M.) should especially pay attention to these co-ops because so many of the companies in those industries now use these partnerships to determine which students will make the best future employees. Many of these co-ops lead to permanent jobs. This provides a significant advantage for students who need a lot of income and enough time for their studies.

While I was in college, I had friends and classmates who would take off a semester of school—or sometimes a year—so they could work full-time and take time away from school. This sabbatical from school usually helped them save money for school, but it also prolonged the ultimate goal of graduating in 4-5 years. Many of them got so used to the idea of making "full-time" money that they developed a false sense of good money habits, all as a result of a lifestyle where they lived according to a full-time-salary budget even though they were full-time students.

Working full-time and going to school full-time is very demanding and time-consuming. During my undergraduate senior year, I worked full-time for a brokerage firm that was a subsidiary of a large bank. My pay was decent for a 23-year-old, but I had already bought my first house from the investments I started my full-time job. I was fortunate because I had a manager who was very understanding, and knew I was trying to complete my college education. I went to school four nights a week and some Saturdays depending on the semester. This was my best-performing college year in terms of my grades, my budget, and my career. I graduated from Kennesaw State University with both the tools and the experience to meet and serve many other students who were like me, by helping them know that I achieved my goal of earning a degree without debt.

Students who choose to work full-time may require commitment to work more than the typical forty hours per week. Many full-time positions, for example, rely upon metrics or performance-based goals, and these demand that students produce a certain amount in a certain amount of time rather than payment based on a set number of hours. The commitment to school and work is almost impossible to keep equal. I had to prioritize school first—before my $22,000 salary job—because I knew I would apply for more positions as soon as I graduated. Presently, the best options include working a full-time job that allows a flexible schedule of flexibility, freelance and contract work, or a job from a family-owned small business that lets you freely negotiate how you will spend your time.

I worked part-time during my first four years in college, but it was difficult to balance working 20-25 hours per week along with studying. I never had enough money or enough time. I worked a lot in retail and had no flexibility in my schedule. Also, the pay was minimum wage ($5.25 per hour). I eventually figured out that all this time, money, and energy was not worth the studying I gave up.

Another option, which is more of a hybrid option, is to work part-time through a work-study program on campus. This is a job that complements your class in spite of its negative aspects. For one, many campus jobs often close down during the school breaks—some of the most ideal times to work because you're no longer in class.

Finally, an option that many students have these days is to work freelance jobs such as Lyft or Task Rabbit. These independent contract companies enable workers to work according to their availability. Even with the positive aspect of having the freedom to schedule your work, the negative aspect is the student must have a car (or access to a car) and adequate auto insurance. Sometimes these requirements make it more costly than profitable since the student will have to maintain their personal vehicle as a commercial vehicle. Having a car and maintaining a car is a major component to consider when you set your budget while attending school.

Roommate and Living Issues

In a previous chapter I wrote about when I had to adjust my living expenses and income after I decided to move into a dorm without a roommate rather than continue to share a college dorm with a roommate. In the latter years of my undergraduate degree however, I moved to an off-campus apartment to share it with a great group of girlfriends. We shared a four-bedroom, two-bathroom apartment, and we all pitched in to pay our expenses. My payment was $210 per month to cover my individual lease, but we were all responsible for covering the electric, cable, and phone bills. For the most part, each person did pretty well to pay each bill on time every month. Three of us were best friends (and we are still very close today), and we did our best to tolerate the fourth roommate. Many times I would return from my part-time job at the bank to notice that some things appeared to be missing from my room. I asked both of my best friends about it and they both immediately explained that the other roommate routinely talk on the phone and to listen to my music on my bed. At least one or two compact discs (C.D.s) would go missing every weekend. Needless to say, this created tension between us, so she ultimately moved out at the end of the semester. I never saw those C.D.s again after that.

This was an example of some of the experiences a student may have while living off campus with roommates. The shared expenses can be better for a student's cash flow as you are able to pay monthly bills instead of an upfront, lump sum each semester. Many students often work while living in off campus housing, so they are able to pay as you go for rent, food, transportation, etc. On the other hand, paying month-by-month can create debt very fast if the student falls behind on making payments, and is one of the main ways students accumulate debt.

Living on campus for a student can build up debt as much as off-campus living, but the convenience of living close to campus ultimately saves time and creates a fun experience during college. When I lived on campus I was able to participate in more activities, connect easily with friends, and have a lifestyle that taught me how to manage a transition to adulthood. But after about two or three years, I was just ready to graduate. Thus, the choice of moving off campus became practical as I saw myself achieving my short-term goal of graduating.

The best living option while in college to save money is living at home with parents or other relatives. This is usually free for most students unless the parents present an agreement for the student to pay specific bills in the house while attending school. My niece, for example, had to pay my oldest sister for the electric bill while completing her degree. Similarly, my mother told me that I would need to pay the water bill and my food expenses if I ever did make the choice to live at home while attending school—a mere drop in the bucket in costs compared to living on campus or off campus.

Each student's circumstance is different. I had one student I tutored in high school (Maria E.) who had four younger siblings to help care for while she was a student. When Maria started, this task became overwhelming. Her grades began to drop and she could not participate in many school activities. After two years of helping with her siblings, Maria decided to get an apartment with two other young ladies and work on the weekends, all of which allowed her to have a more predictable schedule and to concentrate on her studies and school activities.

Another potential conflict of living at home with parents or relatives is that there is usually little privacy, which makes it hard to have friends over or just to study. Some students can function among chaos, but I did not do well in that type of environment. For instance, as a senior in college, I had a full-time job and a few night classes to complete for my degree. I had to go to class after I got off work, but I often had an hour or more before class started. I tried to study at my cubicle at work, only to get interrupted because most of my coworkers thought I was still working. What really helped me was to leave the jobsite and study close to campus at a nearby fast food restaurant. This gave me an additional hour to study, which was especially beneficial before a test or a quiz.

With all my living experiences in college, I believe I gained great insight on how to budget and live a decent lifestyle. I do not believe I could have saved any more money nor done anything different to achieve the lifestyle I wanted—to become a successful student living on campus, off campus, or living at home.

Students and parents will ultimately need to decide the best courses of action for completing school as well the best methods for living on a debt-free budget.

Car Expenses

I was told by my parents—and other family members—to buy used cars instead of new cars because new cars will depreciate over time just like used cars. What they didn't tell me, though, was the problem of having a used car: when you own a car that does not come with a certified pre-owned vehicle warranty, you own a car one level above a lemon! The first three cars I owned had all kinds of problems. It became such a headache to manage a monthly budget and attend school all while praying that nothing new and unexpected would happen to my car. My third used car set the final straw for me. It had an electrical short, so it would not start whenever it rained. By the time I was in college, the car interfered with my class schedule, my ability to get to work on time, and just my basic living needs. This began the next chapter of financial independence.

I gave that car back to my mom. At the time, I was under the impression that she had purchased it for me as a gift. I had thought that she was going to get me a new car if I returned the other one to her, and I was so excited! However, this excitement was short lived as she sold the car and kept the money. (*What?!*)

After that experience, I was faced with a dilemma: to buy or lease a car. In my family, buying a car was considered a major decision. Plus, almost everyone in my family preferred to buy a used vehicle (to avoid monthly payments) than to lease a new car. Since my options were limited, I used Figure 6.2 to consider my options.

Figure 6.2

Buy Used	Lease a Vehicle	Buy a Vehicle	Things to Consider
No money down; low payment	Low monthly costs	Unaffordable on a student monthly budget	Savings was less than $1,000
Repairs unknown	Low maintenance costs	Limited repairs for about 4-5 years	Hard to maintain monthly budget with unknown repairs
No warranty	Warranty as long as the lease	New car warranty	Dependable transportation to school
Less value			Car lifespan lasts beyond graduation

In the end, I decided to lease a new vehicle. This was the most influential decision I made while I attended college. I had one lease payment per month that I had to worry about as opposed to hoping and praying my car would start whenever I got in it. This option also provided the opportunity to budget my monthly expenses around my lease payment.

I went to a popular truck dealership to get a basic truck. Why a truck as a young female? As a student who lived on campus my first few years, I always needed help moving in and out of the dorms during the winter and spring breaks. Many students often changed dorms for reasons such as better parking on campus, better location to major classes, and other conveniences that made life and school a bit easier. My school also required everyone to move out of the dorms every year during the winter and summer breaks for massive cleaning and sanitizing. I went to look at trucks. The car salesman explained the financial plan the company had put together just for college students. The "Good Student Program" was basically a first-time car-buying option for students with "good "grades. I think anyone was eligible as long as you were passing and in good standing at your school. I bought a transcript of my grade point average for that school year to the dealership and was able to pick out a new truck to lease. Thankfully, I qualified. I was also able to show that my part-time job was enough to pay a basic low-level car note. I decided on a basic, small green pickup truck. My lease was no more than $200 per month, and my only expenses were oil changes and tires. (*Whew!* What a load off my budget!)

From then on, I was able to plan a budget that centered on the $200 lease and not have to stress about unexpected repair costs. If I went over the maximum mileage of 10,000 miles in a year, I had another choice to make: to pay for each mile over 10,000 miles, get a new lease, or buy a new car. My choice? I had to buy my own car. (More on that mileage situation later.) Thus, in reviewing my limited options I decided to lease a new, low-cost vehicle my junior year of college. This decision not only benefited me while I was in college by allowing me to focus more on school, but also throughout my twenties after I started my career. This option brought stability and control to my budget, and—best of all—gave me peace of mind.

Today, a car is just one transportation option among many. In some cities, not having a car is the norm and is often more affordable than ownership and maintenance. You can also choose your transportation budget each month with rideshare company options (e.g. Uber, Lyft, etc.). Services like these are easy-to-access and budget-friendly, so they provide an option outside of owning or leasing a vehicle. When I remember that I reserved fifty dollars per month for gas, I think a student today can use that same amount for three or four Uber rides (depending upon your location and travel distance). Public transportation (e.g. bus, taxi, etc.) is still another option that allows students to travel greater distances, enabling them access to part-time job opportunities located relatively far from either their home or their campus—a place where most student jobs may be hard to find since many are already taken.

Things That Can Impact Your Car Expenses

Figure 6.3

Job off campus	Buying a used car	Auto maintenance (e.g. oil changes)	Gas
Sharing a car	Leasing a new car	Auto insurance	Repairs

By the time I graduated from college with my bachelor's degree in business, I had owned four cars and was leasing a vehicle. The four used cars cost me a great deal of money while in college. The best estimate I can remember in terms of repairs, maintenance, and insurance costs my mother paid were about $6000-8000 over 4-6 years of school. There are so many other ways she and I could have used that money to become more prosperous earlier in life.

My husband also learned a lot of lessons about car maintenance expenses during his time in undergraduate engineering school. He owned three cars before he graduated, and he estimates that he spent $10,000-$15,000 on repairs and maintenance over that four year period. He often says if he had to do it all over again he would probably only consider three options: buy a new car, lease a new car, or rely on walking by staying close to campus. Now that he is a professor, he often explains to his students that he would never recommend that they should get a used car. He believes they have plenty of other options and better technology to keep transportation costs down.

I have a family member who currently attends community college. He relies on shared rides and public transportation every day; he budgets no more than $100 per week for his travel to work and to school. He also saves money because he receives discounted public transportation passes through his community college.

Students who are fortunate to have new vehicles or reliable used vehicles can save by buying tires with warranties as well as by comparing the prices of auto parts when repairs are needed. They can also get coupons through online discount vendors (like Groupon) for routine oil changes or local neighborhood auto repair shop deals. To reduce gas expenses, students can also use smartphone apps (e.g. GasBuddy) to compare all gas prices among the gas stations in their local travel area. This also keeps students from driving around—and wasting gas—to find the best gas deals! All these tips are just a small number of ways students can make efficient transportation decisions in order to save and spend money wisely while on a college budget.

I want to share one last lesson about saving on transportation before I close this chapter. My college roommate (Terra W.) owned two vehicles during the four years she attended college, up until she graduated. Her first car was a used car. Just as most parents want to buy something safe, reliable, and economical for their children, Terra's father bought a used car for $1,200 and gave it to her as a high school graduation gift. Unfortunately, the transmission exploded one day while she was traveling on a major highway. Thankfully she survived and was not physically harmed, but her feelings were hurt when she learned later that she would have to help pay for the next car. This created money issues that impacted her budget throughout college. She had to purchase a second car for $170 a month—a large amount for anyone on a student budget. This car note made a college experience quite difficult because she spent much time during the evenings working part time to cover the costs. The good news about all of this, however, was that Terra's car lasted for more than ten years. Even though it was a strain on Terra's budget while she attended school, the long-term benefit was that it helped her finish her undergraduate degree with little to no debt.

<u>Chapter 7: Goals for School Years</u>

Setting goals is important, not only for your years in college, but also for your life and career after college. When I was in school, I had three items that directly influenced my goals: my graduation date, how many years I would be in school, and my degree concentration.

As I wrote previously, a budget for monthly expenses in college is essential. My monthly budget included laundry expenses, car expenses and repairs, food allowance, and other necessities such as hair maintenance—and gas to get to my part-time job. Saving was very difficult to practice regularly, especially early on. My car repairs consumed most of the savings I had put away during my freshman and sophomore years. Once I began my junior year, however, I was able to save anywhere from $50-100 per month. This was a big deal, and it saved quite a bit of money by the time graduation rolled around.

If you are able to save on a monthly budget, try to save an amount that will be sufficient for your emergency needs. Also, try to select a monthly amount that will not impact your monthly budget where you will have to continuously dip into your savings to pay bills. One rule to follow is to save three months of your gross income as a baseline. For example, I made ten dollars per hour at the local bank and worked about fifteen hours per week. This would result in a gross income of about $600 per month, so my baseline savings goal was to set aside $1,800 for an emergency fund. By the time I graduated, I had almost $5,000 saved. I believed I should have had more, but it took me forever to pay off all the debt from all the car repairs.

I finally completed my undergraduate program in six years, earning a degree in business management. Just as my dad had always told me to do what I was good at—instead of what I would I like to do—I chose business administration because I had always been good in business math. In my case, though, I also was able to eventually work in the industry I had always wanted to work in—engineering. I also married a wonderful electrical engineer whose many hours of work have enabled me to live out my dreams through some of his work.

When you set goals for college, the plans will often change as time goes on. It is rare for anyone to follow an exact path of decisions they make from one set of goals. I changed jobs, transferred schools, swapped cars, and moved to new places—all of which were never part of the initial goals I set for myself. Many of these decisions were adjusted based on what worked best at the time for my family.

Overall, I think I made the best decisions I knew how to make in all those circumstances, but if I had to change one thing about my goals it would have been to make the necessary financial sacrifices to pursue my dream of becoming an industrial engineer at the college I preferred to attend. My original college did not offer industrial engineering as a major, nor did it incorporate an environment to my needs with supportive professors, staff, or assets in order for me to graduate successfully. This is only my opinion as all my roommates graduated from my initial university.

My *alma mater*, Kennesaw State University, was a great institution for working students with limited resources who were trying to earn a degree while working full time. My transfer there made the decision to achieve the goal that better suited me. Therefore, I believe the most important goal while in college is to pick the best school that will give you the best opportunity to complete your studies on your greatest interests with the least amount of debt as possible.

Goals Chart

Figure 7.1

Year	Money	School	Career	Personal
1st year – Freshman	Save $25/month	Community college, trade school, or university/college	Work part time; 20 hours or less per week	Achieve a 3.0 GPA
2nd year – Sophomore	Save $50-75 per month	Complete associate degree or start on major classes	Find part time work that relates to your major or in your desired career field	Maintain a 3.0 GPA or better
3rd year – Junior	Save $100/month	Determine major and begin courses for that major	Begin to apply for co-ops and internships	Maintain favorable GPA and join social clubs to network
4th year & beyond – Senior	Save $150 plus per month	Take certification exams. Complete all course work for degree.	Start to interview with companies. Begin to think where you want to work.	Network through business leads, sign up for business networks. Last push for highest GPA.

Money Goals After Graduation

After years of sweat and tears, you finally see the light at the end of the tunnel—the set day of your graduation. Many of your goals have become a reality and you hope to walk across the stage to receive your diploma without owing any money to pay off school debt, but now are also when you need to make goals for the next several years. Do you want to attend graduate school, possibly go into the military, or start your career back at home or move out of state?

After I graduated from Kennesaw, I faced all those decisions, and I started with the safe route: starting a career with the same bank I had worked for when I was a student. It was a stepping-stone, but I eventually left that job to exceed my expectations in terms of growth and financial freedom. I thought at the time I should not continue to wait more than 2 years to get a promotion. Thus, after I cycled through a couple of other jobs, I realized a master's degree would probably give me the best chance to get my desired position and salary in the industry I was pursuing.

It was always a goal of mine to attend graduate school. I compared schools in the state of Georgia, as well as other neighboring states, which all had graduate programs in Public Administration. I set the goal to complete my master's degree by my 28th birthday. Before I started, though, I planned which degree I was going to pursue, how I was I going to pay for school and the cost of living, as well as the type of job I wanted once I achieved this goal.

College graduates who want to complete graduate school immediately after obtaining either an undergraduate degree or a skill certification will need to include an additional budget for at least two years in order to achieve that goal. If your goal is to get the most competitive salary, then the option of a graduate degree plus skill certification (e.g. project management professional, certified public accountant, etc.) is an excellent reason to put off a career for an additional two years.

Another option is to join the military. I strongly considered this option after I met with a recruiter for the Air Force. This was between my fourth and fifth year of college, the timeframe when I felt I was sincerely trying to make a decision that would benefit my long-term future the most. Financially, I was working full time, so I had enough money for my lifestyle, but it was going to be difficult to complete my degree and maintain my standard of living at the same time.

As I thought about the decision, I knew I wanted to earn at least $10,000-$15,000 more than what I was already making, and I wanted to finish within the next two or three years. I was very anxious to start my career, but I also wanted to travel, have retirement benefits, and possibly earn a master's degree. The Air Force, along with the G.I. bill, a benefit that helps Veterans pay for college. This would allow me to fulfill all my goals, all while paying for my education while I worked and travelled.

Once again, I had family influence in the decision. My oldest sister is now retired from the army, so at the time she gave me the benefits and the disadvantages of frequently traveling away from family.

The only reason this choice was not my ultimate decision was because I had other goals I wanted to pursue that would allow me to have more financial flexibility while starting a career. I wanted to invest in real estate and rental properties, for example. I wanted to save in a 401K with a company that would match my contribution, and I wanted to make more money in order to save enough to retire early in my 40s. I also wanted to really give the job market a chance because in a large city like Atlanta, my degree could really make a difference in pay. By choosing this path, I was able to use rental income as my official supplemental income, and I was able to earn the same salary I earned through my job at a telecommunications company. This also provided the opportunity to invest in my employer's 401K. This was the best decision for me, but this option may not work for someone who is looking for more long-term options.

My final option I considered upon graduating college was moving out of state to pursue a career with a high-paying job in a location with a low cost of living, and this actually happened about five or six years after I graduated Kennesaw. (This is an option I wish I would have considered more because I believe it would have prevented the three layoffs in three years I experienced during the Great Recession.)

The opportunity to be mobile can be a great asset when starting your career. It allows you to explore new areas of the country and to give you the flexibility to be promoted to other divisions in different regions of the country, but moving from a familiar city to a new city is much more difficult on a college graduate's budget. For one, if you receive a job opportunity out of town, you must first review and research the cost of living to make sure you have an acceptable salary to afford living in your new city. Then you need to calculate how much you will need for moving expenses just to start work. Also, if you are living in a state that does not have state income tax, it may be a big adjustment to pay local and city income in whichever you state you move to.

Other factors that can affect relocating within your career includes having a family, possibly an increase in car insurance, having a support system nearby, and many other factors that can ultimately alter your life. All these items and much more, have to be considered whether you are just beginning your career or are 15-20 years into it. Hopefully your new company will pay for your moving expenses whenever you get a position out of town or out of state, though this has not been a consistent benefit as it was in the past. Companies today mainly limit their relocations benefits to senior management and executives, so whenever you plan goals for a career after graduating, think of a plan that can prepare you both as a student in college as well as after you finish college.

Chapter 8: Building Credit for Life

Now that you have planned your college goals and your after-college goals, the next step is to build a positive credit history. There are three factors that influence your current and future credit situation more than any other factors, and you will need to consider them when you prepare to build credit. These are student loans, credit cards, and car loans.

Student loans are one of the top reasons most people in their 30's-40's cannot afford to buy their first house. For example, my uncle (a Dean of Pharmacy) once told me his student loans were so expensive that his monthly payment was often higher than his mortgage. Many students use student loans as their first choice for financing their education and living expenses while attending school. You can choose from many different types of student loans including federal loans, personal loans, and commercial loans.

Federal loans are usually determined after students (or their parents) complete the Free Application for Federal Student Aid

(F.A.F.S.A.) application for federal loans. In most cases, federal loans are considered the least expensive to pay back since the interest rates are set by the federal government. Once approved for a certain amount the money can go directly to your school to cover most or all of your tuition and fees. Any money that is left over usually goes to the student to spend on school needs, living expenses, etc.

This is where many students become trapped or even engulfed in debt as the extra loan money is used for beyond education fees. My roommate, who pursued her doctorate in family and children therapy, racked up over $100,000 to complete all of her degrees. She is now able to demand a higher salary, but the burden has shaped all of her decisions—everything from starting her own practice to working multiple places to pay off her loans as soon as possible. Presently, the federal student loan website provides lessons on how to pay for college through a variety of documents and graphs. These are designed to help students as young as middle-school age to start saving for college.

Some federal student aid programs also provide grants and work options such as federal work-study programs. These are not considered loans, so repayment is not required. These grants are specialized in specific areas of needs and/or disadvantages. The Teacher Education Assistance for College and Higher Education program (i.e. the T.E.A.C.H. program) for instance, helps many aspiring teachers and educators with resources to begin a career in teaching. One of the basic requirements includes teaching at least four years at a school that is considered a low-income school or one that is in an economically disadvantaged area.

The loans offered by federal student aid must be repaid. It is important to consider that while the specific types of federal loans provide varying dollar amounts for students with severe financial needs, they often come with fixed-interest repayment rates (e.g. 5 percent over a certain number of years). The Direct Unsubsidized Loan, for example, lends the greatest amount of money—up to $20,500—to students who qualify (based on a variety of factors).

Many of the federal aid programs today are accessible online, which makes for a much quicker process compared to the one I had to endure when I was a student. Plus, high-income students can speed up the application process even more. Many banks offer personal and private loans for students who qualify. These loans usually have higher interest rates that are very similar to credit card interest rates.

A new tool that has recently been made available to students, as an option to pay for student debt or college tuition, is the Income Sharing Agreements (I.S.A.). Schools and universities across the U.S. are creating programs around this finance option for college. There are many moving parts to an I.S.A., but an overview is that it you do not repay more than a certain percentage of your annual salary every year for a predetermined number of years. For instance, you might borrow $10,000 and never pay more than 10 percent interest per year for the next ten years. The percentage, however, is based upon your annual salary, so the amount you pay may fluctuate if you receive a raise each year. Figure 8.1 shows an example of how an I.S.A. is used.

Figure 8.1

Year	Salary/Year	Total Paid for Year
1	$40,000	$3,200
2	$40,000	$3,200
3	$42,000 (5% pay raise)	$3,360
4	$42,000	$3,360
5	$42,000 (Pay Freeze)	$3,360
6	$45,000 (New job)	$3,600
7	$46,350 (8% pay raise)	$3,708
8	$46,350	$3,708

Another moving part is that the I.S.A. depends on your major and the agreement you have with your school.

Again, these options may help students earn an education, but proper planning and budgets are the most efficient ways to ensure students graduate with little to no debt. There are many calculators and informational aids online that can help students to budget and estimate their needs over the time they attend school. Hopefully students will also explore other funding options (e.g. scholarships, part-time work, and grants) before they decide to go with personal loans. It is true that in most instances you should have more funding than you need in order to start a project. Unfortunately, when excess funding is derived from debt, major problems are likely to affect students long after they graduate.

When I graduated with my undergraduate degree, I had already purchased my first home. Many of my classmates did not understand how I had a credit history to qualify for a single-family home. I explained that I could use most of my income for living since I had not acquired any debt (except for a small loan in the amount of $1,000 for books). My debt-to-income ratio was very low, not only because I had no credit card debt, but also because I had paid off all used car repairs debt in full.

Many students do not consider their credit until it is too late—when they need good credit for major purchases. Every financial decision that is made from the beginning of college to the graduation will impact future purchases such as a starter home, a more reliable vehicle, or renting an luxury apartment in another city. Your debt-to-income ratio and credit history can affect all these decisions at least five to ten years after your graduation.

Figure 8.2 is a basic scenario of trying to buy a home after a student begins to pay off their $25,000 school loan debt:

Figure 8.2

Scenario;	Monthly Totals:	Debt-to-Income Ranges:
New job with $50,000 income	Gross income per month: $4,166	Good range: 0-35 percent
Student loans $25,000	Debt payment per month:	Fair range: 36-43 percent
New car payment	Car+Student Ln+credit=$2,000	Least likely to get credit: Higher than 43 percent
Relocating for a new career	Debt-to-Income: 48%	

Debt-to-income ratio is a ratio most banks use to determine if you are able to afford a home loan and mortgage payments. Why is the debt-to-income ratio so important? Most lenders believe that a borrower is more likely to have difficulty paying monthly payments if they have excessive amounts of debt. When I applied for my first mortgage the debt-to-income ratio standard was 35 percent. Of course the ratio of 35 percent is not a fixed number, as many financial institutions will allow flexibility to make a good-faith effort based upon consumer financial rules.

As you start to review options to fund your education, basic questions need answered and plans have to be made in terms of the possible impact these loans will have on your life after graduation. You will want to ask such questions as, am I confident I can finish my chosen major in four years? Do I have enough living funds that don't require me to take out a loan? What work options do I have to supplement my school expenses? Have I exhausted all grants and scholarships before taking a loan? These questions, and many more, will affect your future career, standard of living, and whether you will need to work several jobs just to make a living wage or not.

Overall, loans are a viable option to pay for your education so that you can earn an education to contribute to society. However, if loans are a major chunk of your debt, the payment in the future will ultimately consume most of your income. In that case, the achievement of a college degree will not have as much of a good benefit for your future if your salary cannot pay off that school debt. These choices helped me begin my career at a successful level without starting in the hole of debt before I could make a living.

The next financial decision that can impact your credit is whether to own high-interest credit cards or not. When I was a student, many of my college friends would often open a department store or specialty store credit card to receive an extra discount at the time of purchase. On the front end, they would purchase an item for maybe 20 percent less, but would have to pay finance fees as high as 20 percent over the course of several months. This "discount" is used today as a marketing tool just as it was used in the past. The problem back then was that many of my schoolmates would open several cards and only pay the minimum balance each month. This caused them to carry a balance that continually added more interest each month. The problem is the same now as it was then. This causes your credit card balance to continue to grow so that you owe more at the end of six months than you did when you purchased the original item, far exceeding the original purchase price minus the 20 percent discount!

As an example, see Figure 8.3. If you buy a dress for a homecoming party on campus, and if the interest is compounded daily, then in nine months, you owe more than the original payment ($100)!

Figure 8.3

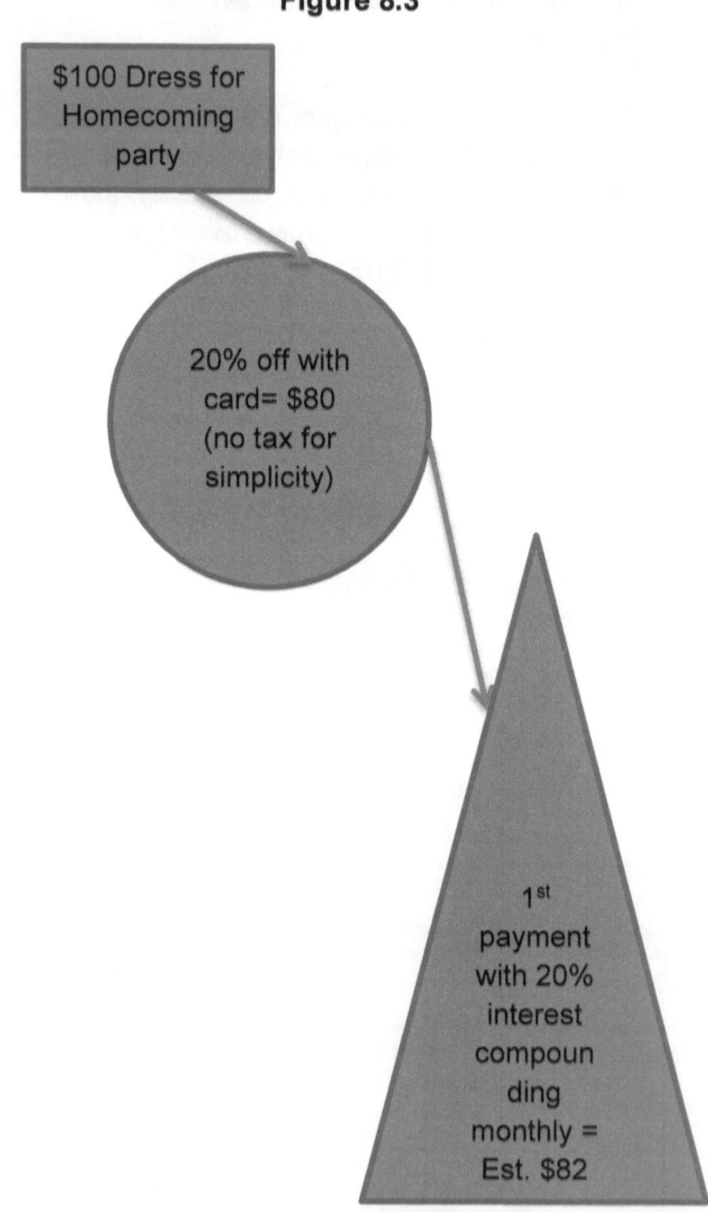

Oftentimes, many students have no choice but to settle with high-interest credit cards when they have little to no credit. If this occurs, I suggest getting a basic credit card at the lowest interest rate possible, and then try to establish credit after about a year by applying for a credit card with a lower interest rate. While you wait in the meantime, however, you should use the basic high-interest credit card for emergencies only.

We all have emergencies. While I had my used cars in college, it seemed like I always had a dead battery, a flat tire, or no oil! Any of these emergencies can happen with a vehicle. Other emergencies can include last-minute fees for class, helping a roommate, or just falling short on cash before the next payday.

The main lesson about managing emergencies and using a credit card is to set a limit for you. For instance, a new outfit for a party may not qualify as an emergency. Also, a road trip to get away for a weekend while in school is not a typical credit card emergency. Don't get me wrong, it is truly tempting to use. It is easy money to access and convenient money to spend when you are ready to have fun. Unfortunately, it can be a decision that will cause a debt that may take 10 times the length of time to pay off than you expected due to the high interest rate.

Keep in mind that most department store credit cards and reward credit cards tend to have higher interest rates than regular bank credit cards. These types of debt not only put your credit score at a disadvantage, but they also stifle your future buying power for a home. They also affect your ability to get a business loan if you want to start a business after graduation.

As you can see, credit history at the time of graduation is drastically important. Many new college grads dream about purchasing a new vehicle as a graduation present for all their hard work. Thus, they begin the process by going to their credit union or bank for an auto loan. As I mentioned previously, I had a leased vehicle and by the time I graduated I decided to lease a second vehicle after my initial lease had ended. This gave me a chance to add to my credit history as well as have a low car payment when I started my career with a small, conservative salary. This also allowed me to concentrate on my new career and not be concerned about repairs or needing enough money to pay an expensive car note.

Many of my other friends were fortunate to have received a new car their first year in college. If they kept their cars in good condition all four years, it was practically brand new by the time they graduated from college. Once they graduated after their fifth or sixth year after beginning school, the new car was already paid off! Thus, they graduated and started their new career with a barely used vehicle with no debt. A plan like this gives the individual much more freedom in their budget. Options such as taking a year off before working full time, travelling for a couple of months, or possibly starting a business become much more affordable.

(Note: Another choice for a vehicle loan is to refinance a high-interest car loan. A good time to do this is right after you graduate and start your career as this will also reduce your total debt while you make your budget for your future life.)

Now that your plans are made and your budget is set, there needs to be time to start putting all the things you learned about money into practice in real life. Also, you need to consider what you have experienced with money while in college to have a concrete plan of action. This action plan needs to be a merging of what you have learned with what decisions you have made while in school.

<u>Chapter 9: Where Should You Be Financially Right Now?</u>

Hopefully, you are now looking towards the light at the end of the tunnel when it comes to graduating without debt. In your last year and last semester of school, you should have some definite choices and planned actions made for your future.

First, you should be able to evaluate if you need more money to finish your degree, or if you are financially stable to graduate on time and on budget. Since plans can change as you get closer to graduation, be sure to ask good questions such as, is there one additional class that is needed to complete your degree that you did not anticipate? Or did an unexpected expense come due the last semester of your senior year? This is a time to review your goals, take note of what you have accomplished, determine how your budget has sustained you all these semesters, and consider what may have to change in order to reach your savings goals and to pay off all your debt by graduation. The big question for your final year is, "Have you accumulated more debt than you have saved?" Hopefully you were able to identify to change your budget and when not to spend more than your savings in order to stay out of debt.

In your senior year budget, you should decide which personal belongings to keep and which ones to get rid of. It is always a good idea to give away what you do not want, or better, to sell it all to your school's underclassmen. This is one more way to make some quick cash to have for extra pre-graduation expenses.

Next, pay any fees or last-minute expenses for graduation commencement. Then, make sure your resumes are sent to desirable positions in the locations you have chosen to live to start your career. Review any leases or dorm requirements to pay any past or late housing fees. You may have to do like my husband did at one point with his off-campus housing; he had an agreement with his landlord to pay her four months of rent plus interest. She accepted the agreement and trusted him to pay her once he graduated and received his first job/internship. He honored that agreement after working during his first internship the summer of his junior year of college.

During my last year of school I owed past due lab and library fees. Many schools will require you to pay all outstanding dues right before graduation, and they often hold your diploma until all those debts are paid. Fortunately, I was able to use my emergency funds to pay for what I owed. I worked continuously during my last semester to build my savings back up after those unexpected fees took a chunk out of my senior year savings budget.

Next, with graduation less than six months away, you need to really study your current finances and any remaining debt that should be paid—or any expenses that will need to be paid—by graduation. This is the best time to accurately identify how much you have in your checking accounts, savings accounts, and under your mattress. My last semester of school I had maybe a couple hundred dollars in my savings, but I remember I did not owe any school fees or old bills. I was starting at close to zero dollars after graduation, but I did have a full-time job and a purchased my first home with money I had saved that was within what my salary could afford.

If you are on the brink of graduating right now, you should already know if you need any resources to complete your education, especially if use banking and budget apps. Presently, many online and commercial banks (and their apps) can categorize your bills, deposits, and savings into categories, making it easier for you set goals for the near and distant future—even through retirement.

After you establish where you are financially, you should be able to determine your next steps as far as working towards being debt free and starting with a good amount of savings to begin your career.

My goals were pretty simple by the time I completed my last semester in school: graduate, have no credit card debt, and have a job that was able to pay all my monthly bills on time. I specify "on time" because many people experience the saga of having more days in a month left over than money in their pocket. For example, your monthly salary is $1,500, but after your rent ($850), your car payment ($450), and your grocery bills and utilities ($250), you are already short on paying bills by fifty dollars! And that may be on the 15th of the month!

My last task in reviewing my finances upon graduation was establishing a chart with a list of questions. This kept me accountable not only to what I had completed up to that point, but also what I had to finish by graduation. Figure 9.1 gives you a breakdown:

Figure 9.1

Where will you be in 3-5 years?
• **Are you happy with where you currently live?**
• **Are you in a town/city where jobs are abundant or scarce?**
• **Do you want to go back to your hometown to start a business?**
• **Do you have family restrictions to consider while looking for a career?**
• **Are you financially able to afford your desired lifestyle in your current city or would your money go further somewhere else?**

Chapter 10: Action Plan … Let's Get Started!

Now that you have a foundation with a budget, a plan, and a completed education in the form of a certificate or a bachelor's degree, you now need to put all of this into an action plan. This plan is needed to execute a successful career and lifestyle for the rest of your life.

As a senior in college, I already worked a full-time job in the investment banking industry. I enjoyed my job, but I also wanted to switch industries because my goal was to increase my income by at least $10,000 per year. At that time, I used networking groups at my university to establish leads to get interviews and meet hiring managers. Students can do what I did, but there are also several other tools available today that help new college graduates find a career in line with their degrees. For instance, the networking site LinkedIn helps you build a network with people from past jobs while also connecting you with friends who can connect you to new jobs. This expands your network to other locations, so this is very beneficial if you are open to relocation after college. (There was a time I thought about relocating, and I even weighed the pros and cons, but more on that later.)

Some other career tools include career counseling and job fairs sponsored by your technical college or university. I went to countless job fairs during my senior year in school. It got to the point where I knew most of the other students who would attend the same job fairs as me! However, it did eventually pay off as I received a job with a telecommunication company which began my career with a great five-year stint. Career counseling usually gives you help on your resume and with job targeting, which directs you to concentrate on a specific career. You may also receive some guidance in selecting and applying for jobs.

It is always helpful to get a professional opinion about a resume. Often the recommendation is to have several different formats of your resume, as this will provide you with the flexibility you need to apply for multiple jobs with a variety of ways to showcase what you can do in light of the specific job details each company is looking for.

I have a friend who graduated from the University of Virginia with a degree in business. He was very focused with his planning and goal-setting; he made it his goal to obtain a job before he graduated, and he even set a specific date as his deadline. He applied for more than 1,000 jobs. Yes, you read that correctly—1,000 jobs! He received 100 or so callbacks and emails and then interviewed for eight or nine positions. After all was completed, he received three job offers that he had to decide on before he graduated. That effort was very rare in those days. In today's job market, on the other hand, this is very normal for the average college graduate. Of course, if you are attending a Tier I school or a highly recognized degree program for your major, you will drastically increase your chances of finding a job right out of school.

Another way to give you a better chance to receive a job right after graduation is by having credible references. A favorite college professor, a manager from a long-term or part-time job, and/or a senior-level coworker who has worked with you for at least a year is all good references.

Also, if you participated in any volunteering opportunities while in college, this can be viewed as a great benefit. With a letter from a non-profit manager or volunteer coordinator, this can speak to your character if you show that you contributed to a noble cause for the experience and not necessarily for the pay. There are countless opportunities to volunteer on college campuses, local churches, food banks, and other charities. I often volunteered for causes that aided the poor, veterans, and people who had medical disadvantages with little access to affordable healthcare. If you are lacking in finding references, this is an option that can provide them.

The next decision of your action plan needs to involve thinking 3-5 years in the future after you graduate (see Figure 10.1).

Figure 10.1

Completed! Yet to do..

Completed!	Yet to do..
Check with school for any past due fees	Downsize any items not needed for living space.
Gather reference letters from professors	Look for job in my field of studies
Pay cap and gown fees with any other commencement fees	Post resume on social media platforms for job opportunities
Check with school advisor to ensure all course credits have been accounted for your degree	Determine if you want to celebrate with a party or just a dinner and budget for attendees

Now that your action plan is taking shape with decisions and choices about relocating and your new career, you need to write down possible advantages and disadvantages of each decision.

My husband's major in college was electrical engineering, which is considered part of the S.T.E.M. field. When he looked for jobs in the area where he grew up, he discovered that the opportunities for electrical engineers were limited, and the ones that were available had lower-than-average salaries.

When I graduated with my undergraduate degree, my career began with a solid path in finance and telecommunications. Then, when the economy had a recession, I had to develop a new action plan because I decided to move to another city that had many jobs in line with my education and skill sets. I first researched the top ten cities that had potential-growth jobs for people with an education in business management as well as an affordable cost of living. Then I narrowed down my choices by considering location to family, the opportunities that I was receiving, and how long it would take to establish a network and get hired

When I had to make this relocation decision, I initially wanted to stay closer to home. I wanted to stay mostly in the southeastern part of the United States. Compared to some of my classmates, who were open to relocate anywhere in the world because they had family members and other unlimited resources in different locations around the world, I had few personal connections. However, I ultimately went overseas for a job through the military—a great, memorable experience I will have to explain in my next book.

The next phase of the action plan is to decide on 3-5 cities you think you would like to live in to start your career. If you are want to reside in the same city where you grew up or where you went to college, I recommend picking three areas within the metropolitan area that have reasonable rent rates and a reasonable proximity to your worksite.

I spent my whole childhood in Atlanta (Georgia), and spent the vast majority of time on the southwest side. When I graduated, I decided to live in a suburb and eventually moved again to the northwest part of the city. This was the perfect decision for my commute to work. It took me less than thirty minutes to get to work even with traffic. I was able to get to work by 7:30 a.m. and get home at the end of the day by 6:00 p.m. The decision also helped me continue to network with recent graduates while establishing my career right out of school. During those years, the northwest area of Atlanta was a major business center. I settled in this area of Atlanta because it provided the best opportunities at the time. I was also able to grow wealth because I lived in a neighborhood that had great value and good access to networking events in the main metropolitan area.

Staying in the Atlanta area meant I could earn good pay, stay close to family, become economically stable, and grow my career— or so I hoped. Within two years of moving to that suburb of Atlanta, I lost my father to pneumonia, got laid off, and graduated with my master's degree. These major events changed my life. I had to reassess my life, including the choices I made with my career as well as the location I lived in—all when I was just twenty-eight years old.

College and technical school graduates have many options today that make it appealing for them to move away from home, including the choice to live within the city, move out of state, or move abroad.

First, if you decide to move within your current city, complete as much research as possible to review how the city plans to develop itself economically over the next 3-

5 years. Also, try to find if any of the major companies that plan to establish themselves in the city offer work in line with your field of study. The, compare housing on an entry-level salary. Will you need a roommate? Can you commute without a car? Do you have student loan payments to factor into your budget? (Hopefully, if you followed your plan and budget laid out in the previous chapters, you won't have any student loans!) Finally, make a list of pros and cons for each city. These decisions will hopefully make your senior year—and your new career—very effective.

<u>Chapter 11: Graduation Day</u>

CONGRATULATIONS!!!!!

You made it! Yeah! You now are awarded a certificate or diploma for your hard work for the previous two, four, or six years (as it was for me) for a technical, associates, or bachelor's degree. Now it's time to really start putting your immediate plans to action.

If you did not receive a job before graduation, now is the time to network assertively and apply for positions. I would set a plan to apply for at least ten jobs a day. I looked for a job like it was a full-time job! I attended career fairs, networking events, and signed up to talk with recruiters when they visited my college campus. I also put myself on a time schedule to see how much time I spent looking for a full-time job in a certain industry and specific location. My plan was to look for internships, temporary jobs, or part-time jobs if I did not receive a job within a month. I recommend you try to get at least a part-time position in the industry and position you desire for full-time work.

Thankfully, I had a job before graduation as I was already working full-time and completing school simultaneously. Unfortunately, I had to work on another plan a few years after graduation because as I mentioned before I was laid off—the first of several employment disappointments. I did find employment again, but more on that will be in my next book.

You have sent resumes and networked with colleagues, now it's time to prepare for your interview. Research the company and the position salary before you attend the job interview. If possible, practice with a friend, roommate, or family member to anticipate potential interview questions. You can easily find many questions online that pertain to that specific position. Try to invest in a suit or business outfit to have a clean and organized appearance for the interview. If possible, try to schedule a time that provides you with the best opportunity to have sharp answers with little to no "brain fog" so that you do not have a difficult time relying on your thoughts.

After the interview, it is always nice to send a handwritten note or an email thanking the manager for the opportunity to interview with you. This is a gesture that can go far if you do not receive the position. For instance, if another position becomes available, the manager may automatically think of you and give you another opportunity to work with that company. This has happened to me numerous times. Other applicants turned down the opportunity, and then I received the job offer (or a better job came open) and they remembered me. I did not even have to interview again, but was given the offer on the spot over the phone.

While waiting to see if you receive a job offer, continue to network and update your resume whenever there is a significant event to represent in your work history. Even though the school year is coming to a close and graduation day is around the corner, networking is really the best way to get an immediate interview. The opportunities that come with networking with the right manager could produce opportunities that probably will not be available to the public. Many jobs listed within a company, in fact, are usually for internal candidates that already work for the company.

When I worked for a top engineering defense contractor, for example, I was often asked by my manager if I knew a colleague from any previous jobs who was looking for a job. This is when I would usually go to my network on a popular networking site and ask if anyone was looking for employment. If I received a response, I would forward my colleague's resume. Basically if the person matched the desired skills, my manager wanted my opinion before he interviewed my colleague. He told me he valued my feedback and that it would help him to determine which candidate to hire. (I always gave my honest opinion, but I would never recommend people if I did not believe they could do the job.) One of my former colleagues was able to prepare for the interview and know more about the position than other applicants who applied from outside of the company because I had been connected to him in the past.

Another way to network is to ask classmates for the contact information of the recruiters and talent specialists who recruited them for their internships or co-ops while in school. Let's be honest: we want to have all the best opportunities before entering our career; however, we need to think realistically and use the networks within our grasp. If you desire to improve your possibilities, try networking at multiple schools. I used to network with other students at other city colleges so I could attend job fairs on their school campus. My husband used his connections with a mentor/professor in engineering school to connect him with a top manager at a leading semi-conductor engineering company, which led to one of his first jobs after several internships.

Finally, you are at graduation day! You have a degree, no debt, and hopefully several job offers. You have created a plan, executed with specific actions, and gained measurable results. Achieving an education is a great effort, and valuable for your journey towards your dreams and goals.

While this is a great time for celebration and having fun with friends and family, real-life responsibilities are beginning. Now you can make decisions and plans based on a foundation that provides opportunities and resources for the next phase of your life.

With the next phase ahead of you, it might be a good idea to use the planning and decision process to start setting goals for the next five years.

I know you are saying to yourself, "I just got out of school! Do I really need to set more goals?" Well, yes! At least start thinking about abstract, top-view goals that you think you will be able to achieve in the next 5-10 years.

During this time of transition, new graduates can pursue a variety of life goals that can span five years or more. For instance, you should decide whether you need to pursue a master's degree to enhance your career. Do you want to be a permanent resident in a house or a condominium? Should you start saving in a company's 401K at the maximum amount that matches your company's contribution? Maybe you will decide to plan the first five years of your career much like I did.

My post-graduation plans for my career began when I reviewed job descriptions on my company's internal career website. I applied for every position I was interested in, and for every position I knew I could reasonably obtain within the next five years. I moved up in ranked positions every 10-12 months.

I started at a low salary. I called it the "twenty-something syndrome." I made about $25,000 per year at the age of twenty-three. I decided to buy my first house at 23 years old for $60,000. My career plan included two job changes that ultimately increased my pay by $10,000 each year, and then I started my graduate degree with my company providing tuition assistance.

I constantly and thoroughly thought through my plan. I executed it almost to the exact timeframe of my plan. I was living the dream! I was a young, single college graduate obtaining goals and resources in expedited form.

Throughout my planning, I never thought anything bad would happen. Looking back, I am very relieved and happy that I decided to pursue my goals by going back to school. (As I mentioned before, I was laid off three times after that five-year plan, and because I had pursued a graduate education, I was able to create a new plan to start a new career.) As I considered whether I should pursue a master's degree, it was not an easy decision to make, because I was living on a small, entry-level salary at the time—mostly working temporary jobs and part-time gigs. My budget was very restrictive for about six to seven years after graduating with my undergraduate degree.

If a master's degree—or something similar—is needed for you to achieve your ultimate goal of a rewarding and successful career, then this is the time to plan for it. This is also the time to plan your budget for another 2-3 years while continuing your education. First, think about researching finance options such as fellowships or jobs that will pay a portion of your graduate tuition. Some employers require their employees to pay for a year of school for every year they work for that company. Others have agreements where they will pay for all of your education as long as you commit to working for them for an extra two years after the completion of your graduate degree. One final option (though it is rare) is to ask for a sabbatical to pursue your next level of education full time while the company keeps you employed and helps you pay your tuition. This is a common practice among civil servant, higher-management level careers, as well as for public university educators. Finally, be sure to think about whether you want to jump right into a graduate degree so soon after graduating with your bachelor's degree, or if you would rather take a break first. I waited a year to go back, and I believe the time off helped me gather a fresh mind and positive attitude.

Earlier we reviewed options for living after graduation. In a two-or-three-year post-graduation plan, you may consider buying a home as a way to start building wealth. Depending upon your desired location, it may or may not be a benefit to have a mortgage payment while you work to maintain a stable monthly budget. On the other hand, you may need to accommodate a new family, build personal wealth, or just have a smart investment for the future by owning your own home.

Your ability to own a home depends on your credit, past job history, and how much you are able to afford for a loan and an initial down payment. Any college debt you still owe will also bring down your buying power, so you will allow yourself and your family to pursue homeownership the sooner you are debt free. It also opens up more opportunities and flexibilities in housing options, especially if you want to move to an upscale apartment home or pay rent for exclusive housing and amenities.

If homeownership is not the best path to build wealth for you and your family, then there are other means to building wealth you can consider. Many new graduates who achieve career positions are often provided a 401K through the company; typically, the company matches every investment employees make in the 401K up to a certain percentage—which is why some people like to call it "free money." If you are in a situation where a 401K is not a benefit—or not provided by your employer—then you should look into other options such as a 403B or some form of a pension plan. Always be on the lookout for anything unique to your industry that provides incentives for you to save more money before you see your scheduled pay.

Chapter 12: Future Plan for Earning Potential

Overall, your decision to graduate debt free with a new view on your future will elevate your earning potential for your future. Right now you are at a good place financially if you have applied most of these lessons, but it is also very wise to think of goals you want to reach over the next ten years, twenty years, thirty years, and on into the retirement years.

Of course, life happens, meaning many experiences can happen so suddenly that even a well-crafted plan cannot prepare for you to handle. Although I had several difficult times, I always bounced back to my undergraduate plan—I planned and managed on a small income and budget. I must confess that although it was difficult initially, my faith and practice of maintaining a budget got much easier once I was able to graduate with my master's degree and mourn the loss of my father.

Options will become more abundant as you work and discover what is best for you. My plans for ten years down the line, twenty years down the line, and even now have changed many times as I received opportunities and promotions. Ultimately, I wanted to own my own business. This required a process and a plan to set goals in order to have financial flexibility, the skills that will enhance my chances for a successful business, and possibly working temporary jobs that will keep money flowing for my livelihood and personal expenses.

There are many options and choices to consider for your long-term goals. Do you want to work for an international company? Do you want to experience overseas travel and employment? These questions and many more, will set the groundwork towards making your long-term plans realty.

Another option in planning for the future is to consider your plans based on your family and where you expect to be financially in thirty years. Is there a possibility to return to school and pursue a subject that would be more meaningful to you or bring joy to your day-to-day life? Will the financial decisions you make after graduating debt free keep you and your family as debt free as possible? Will you have the freedom and flexibility to pursue the career that you went to school to accomplish?

Yes, there are many questions in preparing a plan to organize an ideal future for you. How does this plan of the future bring us back to graduation day, you ask? The choices you make upon graduation are critical to your financial earning power for possibly the next decade.

If this is too much to consider and you are thinking, "I can't think that far," then another possibility is to take smaller steps by setting goals on an annual basis. This should be done in conjunction with a long-term plan in order to monitor your achievements as well as adjust your goals for the next year. This also provides a realistic view of the plans you have made. At this time, you can make better decisions based upon your past year experience (if you don't like your job in corporate America, for example). It may spark questions like, what am I prepared to do to change my job for the next year? Do I like my current work environment? Is this career what I actually want even though I worked so hard for it while studying in college? Did this opportunity produce the financial plans and goals that I desired while pursuing my degree? All these questions can help with your plans and financial goals for the future.

So now I ask, how do you feel about your financial future? We have experienced a grand tour of finances thanks to my childhood experiences, graduating debt free from college, and everything in between. We have learned important money skills every young person should know, as well as how to save and manage money while in high school. We discovered a plan to write a budget for living expenses while pursuing an education and while working a part-time job. We even covered different ways to pay off education debt, including student loans, scholarships, and other methods. We have reviewed which options to consider while researching which school to attend, as well as the types of schools you can choose. Then, we caught a glimpse of plans—and alternatives plans—we can make once we graduate from college. We learned how a debt-free lifestyle affects our adulthood.

Personally, I see how my decisions change ever more frequently, especially as I get closer to my purpose in my life. As I continue to pursue financial freedom, I aim to make the best decisions to achieve the ultimate goals while maintaining a debt-free life.

Resources

1. Financial Student Aid:
   https://studentaid.ed.gov/sa/resources?_ga=2.95019356.1905480191.1535736775-736206089.1535736775#videos-and-images

2. WellsFargo:
   https://www.wellsfargomedia.com/getcollegeready/paying_for_college.html

3. Associated Credit Union. Greenlight card
   https://welcome.greenlightcard.com/acu?utm_medium=affiliate&utm_source=acu&utm_campaign=US-GA--acu%20newsletter---&utm_content=image-greenlight%20049-200-60day

4. https://www.creditcards.com/credit-card-news/canada-how-credit-card-interest-works.php
   By Laura La Rocca. Published January 9, 2018

5. https://www.consumerfinance.gov/
   Ask CFPB/Mortgages updated March 2017

6. www.consumerfinance.gov Ask CFPB/Mortgages updated March 2017

7. www.Creditcards.com , How Credit Card Interest Works, By Laura Larocca; Published: January 9, 2018.

8. www.Forbes.com Be Careful with Income Sharing Agreements (ISAs) to Pay for College; April 12, 2019